READ IT FORWARD

READ IT FORWARD

Linda Kay

With Contributions from
RRISD Librarians

 LIBRARIES UNLIMITED

AN IMPRINT OF ABC-CLIO, LLC
Santa Barbara, California • Denver, Colorado • Oxford, England

Library of Congress Cataloging-in-Publication Data

Kay, Linda (Linda Wiseman)
  Read it Forward / Linda Kay ; with contributions from RRISD librarians.
    pages cm
  Includes index.
  ISBN 978-1-59884-808-3 (pbk.) — ISBN 978-1-59884-809-0 (ebook)
1. Middle school libraries—Activity programs—United States.
2. Middle school libraries—Activity programs—Texas—Case studies.
3. Preteens—Books and reading—United States.   4. Teenagers—Books and reading—United States.   5. Reading promotion—United States.
6. Book contests—United States.   7. Libraries and schools—United States.   I. Title.
  Z675.S3K26   2013
  028.5'5—dc23   2013029491

ISBN: 978-1-59884-808-3
EISBN: 978-1-59884-809-0

17 16 15 14 13   1 2 3 4 5

This book is also available on the World Wide Web as an eBook.
Visit www.abc-clio.com for details.

Libraries Unlimited
An Imprint of ABC-CLIO, LLC

ABC-CLIO, LLC
130 Cremona Drive, P.O. Box 1911
Santa Barbara, California 93116-1911

This book is printed on acid-free paper ∞

Manufactured in the United States of America

Contents

Preface

When we decided to launch a Read It Forward (RIF) program, we knew that we were onto something special. However, after we presented it at the Texas Library Association meeting in 2009, we realized just how vital this reading promotion can be for our students and our libraries. I would not have considered writing this guide except for this amazing response. I have to start with a huge thank you to Blanche Woolls, who never let me stop even though we ran into many obstacles along the way. My wonderful family, John, Thomas, Daniel, and Hannah, has also encouraged me to continue even when I was tired and did not think it was actually going to be a published book. You all make coming home at the end of the day a pleasure and give me the strength and energy needed to do my job. I want to thank my mom who started me reading. Additionally, I want to thank my Ridgeview family—especially Terry Dumas. Without her help, I could not accomplish all that the students and faculty need.

A program such as RIF must have the approval of the administration.

I am so grateful for the support of all of the middle school principals—specifically Dr. Holly Galloway, Ridgeview Middle School principal, who continued to encourage me to write it down for others to simulate at their schools. I would also like to thank our district administration for their support of the program and this book. Even with his busy schedule, Dr. Jesus Chavez took a special interest in this project. I am appreciative of the time that we have been afforded to launch such a fantastic RIF program.

Many of the great ideas and thoughts were shared with me from other middle school librarians in Round Rock. Without their help in the beginning stages of writing, this book would never have gotten started. I am extremely fortunate to work with a fantastically talented group of librarians who are willing to share at all times. Our original group of nine was a great bunch to start the RIF journey with. Len Bryan and Lori Lockwood who have moved onto high school now—we miss you at our lunches but thanks so much for your creativity. Amy Lott and Michelle McLaughlin—thanks for developing great ways to share the books with the students. Cecilia Fuentes, you are one of the coolest librarians ever. Thanks for your encouragement. Laura Stiles—I've said it before and you know it is true—"Once my mentor—always my mentor." Thanks for always answering my questions and not making me feel silly for the asking. Lori Loranger, my unofficial mentor and confidante, you have been such an inspiration to me. Thanks for always being just a phone call away. I will miss being your roomie. Kate DiPronio, you have been such a driving force behind the RIF project. Thanks for talking ideas out with me and bringing your great experience to the table. Thanks to Diane Hart and Charlene Seizinger who help us at the district level.

Finally, we are fortunate to have a fantastic library director who encourages us, stretches us professionally, and supports us in all of our individual programs. I can honestly say that without the support and concern for me professionally and personally from Carlyn Gray, RRISD Library Director, this project would have ended with the chapter outlines. Thank you for everything.

Introduction

Readers . . . life-long readers . . . a nation of life-long readers . . . creating a nation of life-long readers . . .

No doubt our goal as librarians and lovers of the book is to develop the love of reading—that precious joy of getting lost in a book—in all of those whom we serve. The question is how do we do that most effectively and efficiently? Educators have efficiently researched ways to increase reading scores, but this is not necessarily the way to produce those lifelong readers.

Our experience tells us that there is much more to producing readers than just helping them learn to read the words on the page. But, what is that magic bullet? How do we do that? The truth is there is no magic bullet that will reach all patrons in the same way. Every reader needs to be shown "that book" at the right time to develop the desire to read for fun.

Fortunately, there are ways that we can facilitate this process. Librarians spend hours book talking to patrons about their favorites while introducing them to many wonderful stories. In order to combine curricular needs with pleasure reading, school librarians introduce specific titles that complement what teachers are teaching in the classroom. For instance, the librarian book talks titles such as *Number the Stars* by Lois Lowry or *Night* by Elie Weisel when students are studying the Holocaust in history class. Additionally, teachers partner with the librarian to increase overall literacy skills for the students. Science teachers might develop a unit where students are assigned a science fiction title that corresponds with the current topic of study. For example, when students are learning about diseases, they could also be reading *Fever* by Laurie Halse Anderson or *Code Orange* by Caroline Cooney. This type of unit lesson can be very effective in reaching students. Some teachers even model these practices by reading books aloud to their students. Math teachers might choose to read picture books such as *The Greedy Triangle* by Marilyn Burns or a book in the <u>Sir Cumference</u> math series by Cindy Neuschwander to help introduce concepts and show how much fun math can be.

Other students develop this joy of reading when their language arts class reads a single novel. The teacher must make sure the book selected is broadly appealing; and then can help the class enjoy it by having the class read it at the same time as their peers. This makes it a whole class experience, which gives students a shared experience to discuss in the future. These approaches work, and librarians see it daily when the patrons come to the library asking for a book that is similar to *Holes* or *The Outsiders* because they read it in their language arts classes.

All of these approaches mentioned are good and effective in their scope; but in the library, we are always looking for ways to affect the most patrons with our programs. Since the above activities are somewhat limited by the need for face-to-face contact, they can only reach so far.

Like most librarians, those in my district have struggled and searched for ways to expand our reach. What we came up with was the Read It Forward Program. This has been effective for us; it revolutionized our approach. In fact, we feel it is worth sharing with a broader audience, so they too can reap the benefits.

BACKGROUND

Round Rock Independent School District (RRISD) secondary librarians come together once a month at meetings led by our district director. During these times, we are encouraged to collaborate on projects and ideas. We also recommend continuing education possibilities that would help us improve our programs. At one of our monthly meetings, we discussed attending a literature workshop.

Most of the middle school librarians attended the literature workshop. While we were there, we heard others discussing an intriguing program idea. Rather than just handing out books from the library, this program puts the onus on the patrons. The beauty of this idea is that students would pass the books on to each other rather than just receive them from an adult. This possibility was intriguing to us, so we began discussing how we could effectively put this into play.

The traditional techniques of book talking and piggybacking on curriculum are effective and have made a difference in many lives; however, we were looking for something that would provide a piece that was missing in our programming. We concluded that this piece is the collaborative, student piece. Many educators have experienced the phenomenon of suggesting a title that we know they would absolutely love to patrons just to have them snub the novel. However, two weeks later, the same patron walks in the door, begging for the same exact title because one of their friends suggested it. It can be rather frustrating to have that happen, but this is the nature of adolescents. Rather than stay frustrated, we decided to embrace this phenomenon. You see, we were looking for a reading program that provides the passing on of a great book without the red tape of our previous programming ideas. Additionally, we were looking for a program that would be good for our individual school patrons and would also be good as an all-district program.

We have students who may be enrolled in more than one of our schools across the district during the same school year, and we wanted to provide them the opportunity of having a talking point with other middle school students anywhere in the district. We also were looking for a programming idea that would connect our schools through the use of various Web 2.0 tools such as wikis, blogs, video conferencing, and so on. Through the reading of this book, we were hoping to potentially collaborate across the state, nation, or the world.

We literally wanted to affect the world one reader at a time.

DEVELOPING THE PROJECT

Before beginning our plan, we needed to fully understand the concept and see what else was being done across the nation in a similar fashion. Although we did not find information about widespread programs specifically like the one we conceived, we did discover many successful adaptations to the One Book projects. In 1998, the Washington Center for the Book, located at the Seattle Public Library, introduced One Book projects with "If All Seattle Read the Same Book" (Cole). This project launched similar projects in many libraries throughout the country. These projects, began as community-based reading initiatives, usually run during the summer months. Bafile (2009) shared experiences from three schools with successful programs. Saklan Valley School in California read *Farewell to Manzanar* as its first summer reading; Silver Lake Regional High School in Massachusetts read *The Gospel According to Larry* during the summer as its One Book project; Cape Central High School developed a month-long program titled "United We Read" and has read titles ranging from *A Painted House* by John Grisham to *Tuesdays with Morrie* by Mitch Albom. Because these three projects had a great effect on their patrons and the libraries who serve them, we decided to continue with our plans.

The next challenge became deciding what we wanted to achieve and how we could best achieve it. Were we looking for a summer reading program to challenge our students to read over the summer months? Were we looking for ways to bring students to the library during the school year? Were we wanting to focus our attentions in one area? We decided to concentrate on one book throughout the school year because we had a captive audience. Our students and staff would be in school every day, so we would have access to them. We did not want to exclude anyone from the program due to them not being able to attend functions during the summer months, so following the school calendar was the best approach for us due to the fact that we have access to the students during this time table.

After much discussion, we entitled our program **Read It Forward**. This concept is loosely based on the novel, *Pay It Forward* by Catherine Ryan Hyde. In this novel, the main character devised a plan to show a kindness to three individuals that they could not accomplish on their own. Rather than ask them to pay back the kindness, he told them they needed to pay it forward to three more individuals, who would then pay it forward to three more individuals, and so on. Since one of the greatest kindnesses is sharing a great book, this seemed a natural fit. Additionally, we wanted to help provide the joy of reading during the school year while we were most accessible to foster that joy.

Students do not always read for fun during the school year because they are "too busy". It is important that we, as librarians and reading specialists, encourage pleasure reading all of the time. This gives students, faculty members, parents, as well as the entire community the opportunity to participate in activities before, during and after reading the book.

For a program of this magnitude, it is also extremely important to have the support of the major players. For this reason, books were handed out to members of the leadership team, including the principal, the PTA president, the school secretary, department chairs, and others who were encouraged to read their books and pass it on to other members of the leadership before the actual reveal date for the students. By having these people on board before the student books are given, we ensured that these people would immediately be able to start talking about the various points of the book. Plus, they were able to talk to parents, business leaders, and neighbors about the initiative as well.

Once the official reveal date arrives and the books are distributed to students, the adults are already talking about how great the program is and how specific students will enjoy certain parts of the book. Then, the sense of community is stronger, and obvious talking points are made based on the characters in the book.

We chose *Schooled* as our first book, partly because it offered great talking points about what it means to be a good student, a good friend, and quite frankly, a good human being. Because of its antibullying theme, there were many opportunities to talk about how the protagonist, Cap, dealt with the bullies. This made it easier for our students to talk about some of the trials they were personally experiencing. The Read It Forward initiative provided us with the launching point our schools were looking for to build a positive school climate. We were soon proud to proclaim ourselves as a school and a district who reads together.

There were many reasons that we decided Read It Forward was the program that we wanted to implement in our schools. When we decided on RIF as our collaborative reading program, we had multiple goals. First, we wanted to introduce our schools to a great book in order to promote reading for pleasure. It was important that we find a superb and pleasurable book that would be beneficial to each student as well as staff members and parents.

Second, we wanted to promote unity among our individual schools. At the middle school level, students are generally concerned about finding ways to fit in with their peers, and fit into the middle school environment. This time in our students' lives is pivotal to their development. If we as educators can help them find a way to feel a sense of belonging, we need to do so. When everyone is introduced to a single book and this book is literally passed from one member of the community to another, the exercise provides a great opportunity for conversation and shared experiences that can contribute to a unified school climate.

Third, we wanted to provide a clear focus for library programming throughout the school year. Every year, we consider ways to bring patrons into the library so that we can connect them with the resources they need and want. We often have some great programs, but they are sometimes isolated and not necessarily connected with each other in any way other than being held in the library. The Read It Forward initiative focuses the programming for the year. For instance, *Schooled* provided many opportunities to build upon with different activities with students. One activity was to tie-dye and make simple friendship bracelets. The students loved having the opportunity to do something fun and different. What they did not realize is that we were also learning while we had fun. For instance, students learned how to accomplish the tasks to create the crafts. We also discussed the history of these activities as well as how they related to the book. The discussions were much more authentic than if we had just sat down to discuss the book without having an activity structure because the environment was relaxed and focused on a task rather than the discussion itself. This type of activity provides a great way for the librarian to work with students in an informal way that also provides them the time to build relationships with each other.

While you make a bracelet with students, you can talk with them about their home life and things they like to do. This is a great way to see what types of activities they might like to see in the library in the future, and it gives you the information that you need to suggest more reading materials for them as well. By having a book to launch the activities, you can focus on a central theme. This also provides conversation about connections with the book and with life in general, which brings us to the final reason we chose this initiative.

We wanted to specifically connect with academic studies through the library programming. One of our major challenges as school librarians is to provide our direct connection to academic achievement. Even though the focus of this reading program is on pleasure reading, we needed to come at it from all angles in order to reach as many patrons as possible. One way to get students excited about reading is to connect it to the curriculum they are studying. Our experience has been that if the teachers are interested in a book, the students will follow, and vice versa.

RIF was extremely successful in providing a common theme for library activities throughout the school year. For some of us, this was exactly the type of focus that was needed for our individual programs. More than just the library, the school climate was affected because of the theme of the book. We were able to talk with students about acceptance of others even though they might be different from us. Additionally, reading was a huge focus for the campus due to everyone's desire to read the book and pass it on to a friend. The most amazing part of developing a RIF program is the benefits gleaned years after the initial program is over. Even now, there are teachers who read *Schooled* aloud to their classes. Then, the teachers come in to ask for other titles to share with their students. So far, each of the RIF titles has been chosen as a read aloud to share more literature with their students. RIF is the kind of program that will show benefits for years because it is students sharing literature with each other which is the type of life skill that all of us strive to achieve with our students.

PURPOSE OF THIS GUIDE

In this guide, we have laid out a step-by-step program for you to follow, along with examples of what we did and how we did it. It is meant to guide you and your colleagues in establishing your own Read It Forward program, and ultimately, to spread the joy of reading to young people. The examples and experiences that we have revolve around students ranging in age from 11 to 15; however, this program can be used for students as young as seven or eight even through young adults in college.

One aspect of the Read It Forward Program is that nine of us worked on this reading program together, but we all have different personalities with varying strengths and comfort levels. Additionally, our nine schools have various needs and socioeconomic levels. So, we each had to adapt the specifics to what would work most effectively for our populations; and we did. You can too!

Still skeptical about your ability to promote this type of program? Think about this . . . your patrons deserve the best that you can give them. Our nation is in a literary crisis that we as librarians have the power to change. If we can effectively grow a new generation of readers, we are growing a new generation of thinkers; we are growing a new generation that will save our world—one reader at a time.

You have the power to do this:

- Whether you are a librarian who likes to have every piece of a program planned out before implementation
- Whether you are a librarian who flies by the seat of your pants, who may think of the "best" ideas on the way to the event, but can still implement them
- Whether you have plenty of volunteer help
- Whether you have no adult volunteers
- Whether you have access to many financial resources
- Whether you have to scrimp and save for everything

No matter where you fit in this spectrum, you have the power to do this.

Let me share a story with you that I must tell because it is the reason we continue with these reading initiatives. One afternoon, a set of grandparents came into the library to meet me because they had to talk to me before they withdrew their grandson from our school. They wanted to know who hid the books in the hallway. We explained that we hid books for students to find and read as part of our Read It Forward program. This sweet grandmother told us that her grandson had never liked to read until he came to our school. He had only been here about three weeks, but we had somehow gotten him interested so much that he was reading incessantly. Then, she said, ". . . and just think—it was all from a book found in the hallway." I am a crier, so it was not surprising—but tears came to my eyes. If someone else had told me this story, I would have put my hands on my hips and said, "Seriously, one book and now the kid is an avid reader?" But, I did have this experience, and we had seen him in the library every day, asking for book after book after book. Yes, I do believe that one book can make the difference. And, yes, I do believe that a RIF program can affect lifelong reading—one reader at a time.

Please read this manual and implement this program to create a community of people who read because they cannot stop themselves; and because they receive such joy from doing so—one reader at a time.

REFERENCES

Bafile, Cara. "One Book, One School." *Education World: The Educator's Best Friend*. Education World, Nov 26, 2009. Oct 7, 2010. http://www.educationworld.com/a_admin/admin/admin502.

The Big Read. National Endowment for the Arts, n.d. Oct 7, 2010. http://www.neabigread.org/.

Cole, John. "Communities Reading Together." *Library of Congress Information Bulletin*. Library of Congress, June 2000. Oct 7, 2010. http://www.loc.gov/loc/lcib/0206/stateideas.html.

Journal of Adolescent & Adult Literacy. 52. 6 (March 2009): 483(12). *Student Resource Center—Gold*. Gale. Ridgeview Middle School. Apr 15, 2009. http://find.galegroup.com/srcx/infomark.do?&contentSet=IAC-Documents&type=retrieve&tabID=T002&prodId=SRC-1&docId=A196729064&source=gale&userGroupName=tlc139098579&version=1.0.

Lawrence, Salika A., Kelly McNeal, and Melda N. Yildiz. "Summer Program Helps Adolescents Merge Technology, Popular Culture, Reading, and Writing for Academic Purposes." *Journal of Adolescent & Adult Literacy* 52. 6 (2009): 483–94.

White, Thomas G, and James S. Kim. "Teacher and parent scaffolding of voluntary summer reading: voluntary reading of books over the summer can enhance the reading achievement of ethnic minority students and reduce skill loss over the summer break if the books closely match students' reading levels and interests. (Report)." *The Reading Teacher*. 62. 2 (Oct 2008): 116(10). *Student Resource Center—Gold*. Gale. Ridgeview Middle School. Apr 15, 2009. http://find.galegroup.com/srcx/infomark.do?&contentSet=IAC-Documents&type=retrieve&tabID=T002&prodId=SRC-1&docId=A187694272&source=gale&srcprod=SRCG&userGroupName=tlc139098579&version=1.0.

CHAPTER 1
Choose a Great Book

With Contributions from Len Bryan

Your first step when designing a successful Read It Forward (RIF) program is a great book. The book has to be accessible and appealing to all targeted students/patrons. For it to be the most accessible, the book must have the following characteristics: broad student/patron appeal with strong female and male protagonists, a strong plot, literary merit, age appropriateness for the intended audience, programming possibilities, and curricular connections (if for school audience). Another important characteristic is that the author be prolific, with other titles widely available. Although not essential, this aspect was important to us for our first RIF program because we wanted the opportunity to recommend more books written by the author.

BROAD APPEAL

The concept of RIF is for someone to read a great book, and then pass it on to a friend, who passes it on to another friend, and so on. If the program is a success, a large percentage of the community will have read the book by the conclusion of the program. To increase the chances that everyone will read the book **and enjoy it**, the book should have a broad appeal. One way to ensure this is that the book has strong female and male protagonists. The best choices will have both, so that the readers can identify with the characters. However, research has shown that girls are more likely to read a book with a male protagonist than the other way around; so, if you need to choose a book with a single protagonist, a male is preferable to a female.

Some other factors that might help ensure you have a book with broad appeal will be discussed more fully—for example, choosing best sellers that became this category because a movie was made of the book. For younger readers, the Lemony Snicket books are an example of this type.

STRONG PLOTS AND THEMES

In addition to considering the strength of characters, you will need to find a plot to which the students/patrons can relate. Books that incorporate current events in their plot or, as stated earlier, that have been or will soon be made into Hollywood movies are often good choices. If it is an Olympic year and your students/patrons love the Olympics, consider a sports book such as *Gym Candy* by Carl Deuker for high school students or *Heat* by Mike Lupica for middle school students. If students/patrons enjoy going to the movies, a possible choice could be *The City of Ember* by Jeanne DuPrau, *Stormbreaker* by Anthony Horowitz, *Coraline* by Neil Gaiman, or *Guardians of Ga'Hoole* by Kathryn Lasky.

If you have the opportunity, choose a RIF book that will be adapted to film in the future; this becomes instant promotion. Use the film industry's resources, such as movie trailers, to choose a book with a broad appeal. I am guilty of resisting reading *The Guardians of Ga'Hoole* because warrior owls did not sound interesting to me until I saw the movie trailer. Now, I have read the book and cannot wait for the movie.

LITERARY MERIT

For your program to have credibility, it is vital to find a book that has literary merit. One way to ensure that a book has merit is to choose a book from a recognized awards list. Of course, a great RIF book does not necessarily need to come from an awards list, but they are excellent sources. The divisions of the American Library Association (ALA) have several awards lists that are compiled annually. Those lists—if you are not familiar with them—are posted on the ALA website (http://www.ala.org).

Some of the awards listed include the John Newbery Medal, given by the Association for Library Service to Children (ALSC), for the "most distinguished contribution to American literature for children." The Young Adult Library Services Association (YALSA) gives six awards: the Michael L. Printz Award for literary excellence in young adult literature, the William C. Morris YA Debut Award for a debut novel, the Odyssey Award for the best audio book produced for children and/or youth available in English in the United States, the YALSA Award for Excellence in Nonfiction honoring the best nonfiction for young adults for a November–October publishing year, the Alex Awards for the top 10 books written for adults but having a wide appeal for young adults aged 12–18, and the Margaret A. Edwards Award given to an author whose body of work has been popular for a certain period of time, specifically focusing on helping adolescents become more aware of their role in society as they gain a better understanding of themselves. Awards that focus on diversity include the Coretta Scott King Award chosen by the Ethnic & Multicultural Information Exchange Round Table (EMIERT) and ALSC's Pura Belpré Award, established to honor a Latino/Latina writer and illustrator whose work best celebrates Latino cultural experiences in literature for children and youth.

In addition to the previously listed awards lists, several book lists are developed by YALSA to highlight the various outstanding books in a given time period. The lists are helpful in covering a range of interests for the given audience. Published annually are Quick Picks for Reluctant Readers, Great Graphic Novels for Teens, Popular Paperbacks, the Teens' Top Ten list, and the Quick Picks list.

The Quick Picks list is specifically designed to identify the books that would appeal to young adults who do not like to read, known as "reluctant readers." The entire consideration list is published along with the narrowed down list of the top 10. The Best Books committee chooses and annotates books of notable interest published in the previous 16 months. In a similar fashion, the Quick Picks committee narrows their list to the top 10. The Great Graphic Novels list highlights outstanding graphic novels and illustrated nonfiction titles for a given publishing year. The Popular Paperbacks list focuses on books that would specifically promote pleasure reading. The last list is the Teens' Top Ten list, which is entirely nominated and chosen by teens for teens.

Along with the many national lists, most states have lists that are valuable resources for finding the right book for students/patrons. For instance, Texas has the Armadillo, Mockingbird, Bluebonnet, Lone Star, Maverick, and Tayshas lists. To find each state's lists, visit the state library association's website for more information. To find these addresses, search this site at http://www.librarycon sultant.com/associations.htm. A fairly comprehensive list of the various state reading lists can be found at http://teach.simonand schuster.net/state-awards/.

In addition to reading the aforementioned lists, look for titles in review journals and websites such as Booklist, LMC, VOYA, Horn Book, and ALAN Review. These lists can be very informative; many of these can even be found online through sites such as Barnes and Noble and Amazon. Working with faculty, particularly English teachers, can serve your purposes as well since many teachers are avid readers. Finally, professional listservs are a good way to solicit recommendations from people across the globe.

We chose a book from the Texas Lone Star list for our first year. This proved successful, as it gained us access to many prepared resources, and it helped us confirm the choice of book. It is reassuring to use a novel that has already gone through a state committee's scrutiny.

AGE APPROPRIATE

When promoting a book as a good read for all of your students/patrons, it is vital to consider the age appropriateness of the title. A good guide is to aim for the middle age range of your students/patrons. For instance, if the students/patrons are in grades 6–8, choose a book that is great for seventh graders. This will help ensure the book is not too mature for sixth graders, but not too immature for eighth graders. For an elementary audience, it is better to choose a book for the upper grades, and then ask the teachers to read the book aloud to the younger students in the school. Another solution is to run the program with two books that have a similar theme and programming options—one for upper grades and one for lower grades.

In a public library setting, consider taking a vote to choose your title. Ask for suggestions, vote on those titles, or choose a variety of novels and have the interested patrons vote on their favorite. The Pflugerville Public Library in Pflugerville, Texas, has chosen an interesting approach for their reading program. They chose *The Wonderful Wizard of Oz* that has multiple versions and have told people that they may read any of the versions. This is a great idea to bring different generations together. Adults could read the original version or an alternative version, such as *Wicked: The Life and Times of the Wicked Witch of the West* by Gregory Maguire, while children could even read a picture book version such as *The Wonderful Wizard of Oz: A Commemorative Pop-Up* by L. Frank Baum and illustrated by Robert Sabuda.

PROGRAMMING POSSIBILITIES

With a little imagination, *any* book can provide a wealth of programming ideas, but some lend themselves to varied programming more than others. Consider the themes of books that might be good candidates, and compare the possibilities that lend themselves to your talents and those of your staff and volunteers. Also, consider partnering with neighboring libraries. For example, a school library could partner with the public library to serve the entire community or vice versa. If a public librarian is going to carry out a RIF program during the summer, consider partnering with school librarians in both public and private schools. If a public librarian is to conduct a RIF program during the summer, partnering with school librarians before the summer begins would be a great way to publicize the program. Finding partners who can share ideas as well as resources is a creative way to enhance your possibilities.

If a close, physical ally is not an option, then join a listserv such as LM_Net and recruit some virtual allies. This will present opportunities for possible Web 2.0 programming during the RIF program.

CURRICULAR CONNECTIONS

In a school setting, a RIF program will win much support from administration, faculty, parents, and the community as a whole if the book can easily be connected to curricula. For example, *Life as We Knew It* by Susan Pfeffer can be connected to math, science, social studies, language arts, and fine arts in the following ways:

Math—Prepare various survival scenarios that would connect to what the math classes are learning at the time.

Example:
Predict how long supplies will last, based on how many supplies are available and how much is consumed in a day. For instance, with 300 gallons of water and the use of 1 gallon a day to cook, 2 quarts a day for drinking, and 5 gallons a week for laundry, how long will the water last at this rate? Or, use food items and ask the following questions: How much food do I have and how much does each person consume in a day? How much food should be eaten daily if the food must last a designated amount of time?

Science—Focus on weather and climate changes.
Examples:
Properties of volcanoes: Could ash fill the air from so many miles away? What is the role of the moon in our weather patterns? What technologies do we take for granted?

Social Studies—Use Socratic questioning as a technique to discuss with students about individual responsibilities versus the role of the government in the wake of a natural disaster.
Examples of Socratic Questions:
Did the government do a good job of responding to the needs of the citizens? From a historical perspective, did the systems in place improve between Hurricane Katrina and Hurricane Rita and then to Hurricane Sandy? How does school continue when the building is used as an emergency shelter?
Enrichment Lesson:
Develop a safety plan for your house or the school. From a world perspective, there are places in the world where people are surviving without our necessities every day. Do we do enough to help the world? What would you miss most if you were stuck in your house with limited food? What are the differences between the generations that are alive today?

Language Arts—Focus on various literary elements, such as characterization and theme.
Examples:
How did the characters prioritize their survival? Which theme best fits the book? Which character do you identify with most?
Connect with the short story, "Summer without the Sun."

PROLIFIC AUTHOR

Reading the RIF book often leads to students/patrons wanting to read other books by the same author. Selecting a book in a series or the promise of the series as forthcoming will often encourage students/patrons to read additional books in that series. Choosing the book of a prolific author whose other books are widely available broadens the chances of the students finding other books by this author enjoyable.

SUMMARY

As stated earlier, we chose a book from the Lone Star list for our first year. We chose *Schooled* for our first RIF because it was written in small chapters, told from alternating points of view. This will increase the broad student/patron appeal for students participating in our statewide program. This choice further confirmed our literary merit requirement.

It was accessible to our sixth-grade students, but the protagonist is in the eighth grade. Therefore, our older students could identify more readily with Cap because they were the same age. Because it was on the Lone Star list, we had resources prepared by the Young Adult Round Table Lone Star committee of the Texas Library Association that we could use for the program.

In choosing a prolific author for our program, we chose one who had written many other novels as well. Gordon Korman, author of *Schooled,* has more than 40 published books in a variety of maturity reading/audience levels.

For our first RIF program, we discussed several books that were on that Lone Star Reading List. Among the several books on the list that we considered were *Beastly* by Alex Flinn; *Brothers, Boyfriends, & Other Criminal Minds* by April Lurie; *Breathe: A Ghost Story* by Cliff McNish; *Chance Fortune and the Outlaws* by Shane Berryhill; *Zen and the Art of Faking It* by Jordan Sonnenblick; and *Epic* by Conor Kostick. Although any of these would have been a good choice, we were looking for a book that would meet all of our qualifications. Most of the authors of these books had only published a limited number of books at that time. Additionally, we thought that a realistic book would be the best choice so that we could have connections with our curriculum and the types of character qualities we wanted to promote. In the end, *Schooled* fit those qualifications, along with an important one for middle school—short chapters. For our first program, we wanted to be able to work with teachers to promote this as a quick read for anyone to be able to attain the messages.

CLOSING

Finding the book that will best meet the needs of your students/ patrons for Read It Forward can be the most challenging portion of the program. Choosing a book that has broad appeal, literary merit, programming potential, and connections to the curriculum and that is age appropriate will help ensure a successful program. It may take some time to research, but your efforts will be well-rewarded.

CHAPTER 2
Obtain Buy-In

With Contributions from Lori Loranger

For a program such as Read It Forward (RIF) to be successful and achieve its full potential, gaining the support of the major decision makers is key. In our first year, we met as a group of nine librarians to make decisions about the title, programming, implementation, and so forth. Having a planning committee was one of the major components that contributed to the success of our program. We were able to discuss the various obstacles that we foresaw and found ways to overcome them. Putting together a committee that wants to see literacy soar in your community can be vital to the program.

As mentioned in the introductory chapter, even if you don't think that you have all of the talents and abilities to put this program together, someone in your community has those that you don't have. Seek them out, and ask them to be part of your planning committee. Although it is not impossible to implement a program like this alone, it is more difficult. Unfortunately, many of us have worked on projects by ourselves while not giving others the opportunity to explore their ideas and talents. Seek out those who may not have had the opportunity to work on a committee but have great potential. You'll be glad you did.

ONE TEACHER AND ONE VOLUNTEER

Some of the people you choose to help are obvious choices, but some are not. A school librarian who has a very busy reading teacher might choose a teacher who is not usually associated with teaching reading, such as a music teacher or a physical education teacher. However, those teachers may surprise you with their ideas of ways to promote your program. School and public librarians might choose a mom who volunteers in their library weekly and who is looking for a way to become more involved with your project. While it is great to choose one or two committee members who have not had much exposure to your environment in a leadership capacity, it is also important to choose members who have experience. Providing the balance is the key when choosing a good committee.

Once your committee is in place, decide what will be the best way to gain the necessary buy-in from the various decision makers. It cannot be stressed enough that before beginning a communitywide reading initiative, it is essential to get support from the principal players.

PUBLIC LIBRARY BOARDS/TRUSTEES AND SCHOOL BOARD MEMBERS

If you are a public librarian, you will need the approval of your public library/trustee boards. Begin with gaining the approval of your director, who will then help convince the library board. As a public librarian, you want to show your worth to the community through increased use of the collection and programming in the library. This program will draw children and teens to the library without extensive programming.

If you are in a school district with library coordinators at the district level, they will be able to help gain school board approval of the program. If your district has no one at the district level who manages school libraries, you need to make sure that the principal is in agreement with the importance of the program and will help you present the library to the school board.

PRINCIPALS

School principals want to develop a school culture that sustains excellence in education and promotes continuous improvements in literacy. Student success is often attributed to principal intervention and practices. That is their job, after all, as the educational leader on campus. The principal needs to be convinced that this project will be useful for the entire school.

Take a teacher with you when you meet with your principal. This individual can help explain the value of this project to the school. With preparation, school and public librarians can market a city-wide or a school/districtwide reading program, such as RIF, to their library directors and their principals.

Determine exactly what the directors or principals will require or ask prior to making an appointment to sit down with them for an in-depth discussion. Will these administrators want a detailed, written analysis with a step-by-step description of everything; a short e-mail outline of the basic plan; or something in between? Whatever their management style or their thinking about programs within the school, provide the level of detail necessary to make it happen. Share the names of members of the committee, other libraries and librarians who are involved, the title of the chosen book, and the anticipated budget needs for the project, especially those things that these administrators might be able to provide. It is always helpful to show other monies that have been received and the sources the project committee plans to approach for help with funding. At a minimum, ask for permission to go forward with this program, which will be highly visible on the campus and or at the public library. This is important to you and your students/patrons and should be given the discussion time it deserves. These administrators will then evaluate the project in terms of the other activities being planned within the school or public library.

When the project is approved, use this information when your committee meets with other librarians or library groups such as Friends of the Public Library or the school's student council to seek funding.

With your plan in writing, make an appointment to sit down to discuss the RIF program with those whose approval you are seeking. Do not try to catch them in the hallway or when they are busy with another issue. Within the school, you may be asking for budgetary or other campus resources. At a minimum, you are asking for your principal's permission to go forward with a program that will have visibility on your campus and should be given the discussion time it deserves.

In the meeting, outline the general idea of RIF. Let your principal or director know about the book and movie, *Pay It Forward*, on which the program is loosely based. State that the love of reading is one of the most important gifts educators can give their students. Be upfront about the cost of books, promotional items, and program materials. Ask to brainstorm ideas about funding these purchases.

As a public librarian, this program may be used as a summer reading alternative, or your efforts may be to support a school district initiative by making sure copies of the chosen book are available. If your decision is to carry out the project on your own, decide to use some summer reading funds or ask for additional, special funding for the project if you think it may be available. You may also be able to tap your Friends Group to raise funds, but if you do this, be sure to go through the director.

If you are persuasive, and lucky as a school librarian, your principal may offer to cover the cost through campus funds or offer alternative suggestions, such as the PTA or a campus site-based committee. Once your principal becomes involved in planning how to pay for the program, they have mentally accepted it as good for their campus. Likewise, once the public library director is involved in planning, your chance of being able to enlist others is ensured.

OTHER TEACHERS, OTHER VOLUNTEERS

Teachers view librarians as collaborative partners when that behavior has been modeled by the campus principal. Once your principal has bought into the concept of RIF, move on to the staff. Let them know about the program by promoting your plans at a faculty meeting; send an e-mail to teachers giving further details; and choose several colleagues who are already library supporters to receive an advance copy of the book. Ask them to read it over the summer, and pass it on to other teachers/staff at the first faculty meeting of the new academic year.

If you are a public librarian, don't let that discourage you from collaborating with school librarians and teachers. Reach out to your local school librarian, and see if you can get things started.

When volunteers see the value of a program to the school or public library, they may ask to extend their services to this project. The more the members of the community who become involved, the greater is the likelihood that this project will mushroom. The first group in any school is the parents.

PARENTS

At the beginning of the program, ask your principal to send out information to the parents using their normal communication tool—weekly e-mail, e-newsletter, paper newsletter, and any other way news goes home. Public library directors might compose a letter directed to parents in the library newsletter or on its website. You can fully expect that some parents will ask to borrow the book or purchase a copy so that they can read it, so be sure you have sufficient copies to meet this need. After all, we are all looking for something to talk about with our 'tweens and teens and here is a readymade conversation starter.

It is in the best interest of the school for librarians to step out of the library and become involved in schoolwide programs that increase their visibility on campus. Likewise, public librarians need to reach out to others in their communities to increase the value of their libraries. A schoolwide or communitywide reading extravaganza that is fun and educational is an excellent way to do this.

EXAMPLE OF PROPOSAL SUBMITTED TO CAMPUS SITE-BASED COMMITTEE

Site-Based Advisory Committee

Library Proposal

Read It Forward!

Purchase: 100 copies of *Schooled* by Gordon Korman

Cost: $500 (paperback will be available on August 26, 2008)

Impact: This program could potentially impact every student in Cedar Valley Middle School. Realistically, the goal is to have the book passed on five times prior to the author visit on January 30, 2009, reaching 500 students.

Goals: **District:** No Place for Hate; district-wide blog

Campus:

Social Studies: cultural awareness and appreciation; graphical information (survey of cultural background of students/graphing of survey results/early release day program—food from student cultures)

Language Arts: award-winning books/authors; genre studies (book talks/book discussion groups/author visits)

Science: scientific concepts of observation, comparison, analysis, and prediction (library webpage problem-solving brain boosters, links to curriculum-related sites)

Mathematics: graphical representations; collecting, organizing, displaying, and interpreting data (survey of cultural background of students/ graphing of survey results)

Technology: Information transfer between media (blog/library webpage/ presentation media)

Art: (early release day program—tie-die shirts, headbands/beads)

Music: (early release day program—music from the 1960s/1970s on record player)

Program Description: Each middle school librarian in the district will obtain multiple copies of *Schooled* by Gordon Korman and passed them out to students with the understanding that when they finish reading the book, they will pass it on to someone else in the school community. Our hope is that this will provide a wonderful opportunity to talk about tolerance and respect for everyone, including ourselves. This book was chosen because:

1. it appeals to both boys and girls
2. its theme has wide appeal
3. it follows district No Place for Hate goals for teaching tolerance

The reading of a book will be heavily promoted in each school using a variety of methods. A district blog/wiki will be established, where all students are encouraged to share their thoughts with students from other middle schools in the district. The culminating event is a visit by the author, Gordon Korman, on January 30, 2009, which will be attended by all students who had demonstrated that they had read the book.

CLOSING

This chapter has pointed out the need to engage interested parties, both inside and outside the school or public library. This would include colleagues in both school and public libraries, administrators, teachers, parents, and volunteers; and it has made suggestions for ways to make this happen. The next chapter covers ways to acquire copies of the book.

CHAPTER 3

Obtain Copies of the Book

With Contributions from Kate DiPronio

After choosing a book for a Read It Forward (RIF) program and securing funding, the next step is to find a source for multiple copies at a reasonable price. This may require calling and/or emailing vendors, but chances are they will be happy to help with discounts.

In the beginning, this task can be given as a specific assignment to a committee member. If there is someone on the committee who is a good negotiator, have that person contact the vendors to see what deals can be negotiated. If multiple libraries are collaborating on this project, it is best if one person coordinates the book purchase process for all. The more books that can be purchased at a time, the larger your discount will be. Free shipping may also be an option to help with your costs. The greater the buying power, the greater the potential discount.

First, contact local bookstores. They wish to maintain a good image in the community and will work with librarians to obtain multiple copies of a book at a discounted price. Plus, it may be possible to purchase the books at the store and save shipping costs. Each Barnes and Noble bookstore has a Community Relations Manager whose job it is to work with community groups, including schools. Additionally, the coordinator can take sales in each location for author visits. You can find Barnes and Noble store listings at: http://store-locator.barnesandnoble.com/storelocator/stores.aspx?x=y&r=1.

Perhaps you can include their name as a sponsor on publicity materials or signage. If you can offer them some kind of publicity in exchange for their cooperation, you both will benefit. If this option is available, it will also provide a good contact for future events.

Second, if the chosen book will be available in your next book fair, contact your book fair representative about discounts for multiple copies. Scholastic offers a 25 percent discount directly to librarians on books that will be showcased in book fairs. They will deliver the books at no charge if you are on a frequent route for their driver or if there is a book fair currently scheduled in your area. You can telephone Scholastic Book Fairs at 1-800-792-2002 or find them on the web at: http://www.scholastic.com/bookfairs/.

Short on cash? Scholastic will allow your books to be taken as part of your profit from your book fair if they carry it. This is a great option for libraries that choose to take their profits in books. Another option is to partner with teachers who have received bonus points from students purchasing books throughout the year. If they have points available, they might be willing to give free books to the RIF initiative.

Finally, go directly to the publisher. They often enthusiastically work with librarians to promote one of their authors' works. Many publishers also offer large discounts in conjunction with an author visit or a particular reading program. This may take more searching to find the appropriate person to contact. Start by looking inside the book or by finding the publishing company online. Write to the address on the verso of the book and it will eventually make its way to the proper person. E-mail addresses for many publishers may be obtained at AcqWeb's *Directory of Publishers and Vendors*: http://www.acqweb.org/pubr.html.

For authors not residing in North America, try AcqWeb's *International Directory of Email Addresses of Publishers, Vendors and Related Professional Associations, Organizations and Services*: http://www.acqweb.org/email-ad.html.

It cannot be stressed enough how important it is to obtain the books early to allow time to prepare them for distribution. For school librarians, it is ideal to receive the books for the next year's program before the previous school year ends. This ensures that the books are available and ready when the next year begins, and you have them in plenty of time over the summer break. With *Schooled*, we wanted to get paperback copies, but they were not available until August 2008. Since the cost savings was significant, we decided to wait; however, this presented a burden in terms of getting them ready for distribution because of other duties at the beginning of the year.

More information about distribution follows in subsequent chapters, but keep in mind that the most successful programs require time to get the books ready for maximum benefit. Obtain them in May and spend the time making other preparations before summer vacation begins. You will reap the benefits when you return to school and have that task out of the way.

Another consideration is properly storing your books for the summer if you are lucky enough to get that done. Make sure that the books are boxed up and labeled clearly. Put them in a place that will not be bothered by anyone. You may want to keep the title a secret until the reveal date, so consider labeling the boxes in such a way that will alert you that the books are inside without having READ IT FORWARD marked in a black Sharpie on the side.

If you are in a public library setting, you might take the opportunity to prepare the books for distribution, box them in large boxes, mark them clearly, and use that as one of your promotions of the initiative. Experience tells us that people can hardly resist the curiosity that an unopened box provides. Clues can be provided on the side of the box to get patrons excited about the title. School librarians could do this as well if there is space where students could not accidentally open the box. If storage is an issue for you, and you think that storing the books until you are ready to distribute them will be a burden, then stack the boxes together and cover them with a plastic tablecloth or butcher paper. Place a sign that says COMING SOON on it and let that serve as a promotion.

CLOSING

Once you find the best financial deal and your books are purchased, the possibilities for making the most out of your storage obstacles are endless.

As I sat in the library during summer school, I overheard one girl read aloud to her classmates a bit that she had written. It fits this situation, so I will share it with you. "When life gives you lemons, take them to the grocery store and sell them to someone else. Then you can buy what you really want." Take a storage issue and make it into a great promotion.

See, I told you that you have the power to do this.

CHAPTER 4
Promote Excitement

With Contributions from Cecilia Fuentes

No program is successful without ample promotion. To win community buy-in, you must generate a buzz by harnessing the resources readily available. These resources fall into three distinct categories: Bricks, Clicks, and Flicks. Use all of the means and resources at your disposal.

BRICKS—TRADITIONAL RESOURCES

You are likely familiar with the techniques and venues used here, but they bear repeating. For the first, plan face-to-face presentations for your administration, staff, and students. You likely have already spoken to your administrator and fellow staff members; but consider holding a more formal meeting where you make a PowerPoint presentation that presents your objectives and outlines the process of the program. Take the opportunity to recruit more volunteers for any tasks you might need help with later. For example, if you're looking for someone to design, print, and distribute a flyer, this is a great place to ask for help.

With students, you can approach them one-on-one, or in small groups, such as book clubs. If you have a Teen Advisory Board (TAB), be sure to include them in the planning. You may even want to solicit their input on book selection. Older students often enjoy participating as volunteers as well. For example, some may want to help create a website or blog for your program or help design a poster or signage.

Below, you will find an example of the agenda used at a meeting with a building principal. It can be adapted to meet your situation.

Meeting Agenda Items

The agenda items for the first group, your administrators, will present a description of your program plans, the benefits for your students, the budget, and the timing. This will be the best opportunity you will have to sell your school community on this project, so you need to have it well outlined and you must be ready to answer questions.

DESCRIPTION OF PROGRAM

The Read It Forward program has the potential to change the way books are read in our community. This concept is loosely based on the novel *Pay It Forward* by Catherine Ryan Hyde. In this novel, the main character devised a plan to show a kindness to three individuals that they could not accomplish on their own. Rather than ask them to pay back the kindness, the boy told them that they needed to pay the kindness forward to three more individuals, who would then pay it forward to three more individuals, and so on. I consider one of the greatest kindnesses is sharing a great book, and I want to do that for the children in this school. It is important that we encourage pleasure reading all of the time. This gives students, faculty members, parents, as well as the entire community the opportunity to participate in the reading of one book, thereby having a wonderful shared experience.

BENEFITS OF PROGRAM

1. This novel will provide us with shared experience for the whole community. When parents don't know what to talk about with their children, they can use the book as a launch. Private jokes can be about parts of the book. For instance, it would be fun to have VOTE FOR CAP buttons, especially if this is during an election year. For new students, this could give them something to share with the other students when they might be shy and not know how to approach others.

2. *Schooled* was a great book to start a program like this because it was a great reiteration of school goals. We want to promote unity and acceptance of everyone, no matter what their differences may be. We are also very concerned with bullying at the middle school level. *Schooled* provides great lessons on both sides of the bullying issue. The students

who are engaging in bullying behaviors see what needs to be done. Cap also provides a great example of not letting those bullying behaviors get the best of him. He is able to persevere through trying circumstances, never backing down from his beliefs.

3. This book's theme relates to our students' lives because most students have been teased and relate well to the fact that the characters in the book want to fit in. This is especially true of the boy who had been bullied more than any other. Even though he has been bullied in the past, he seizes the opportunity to heap the teasing on someone else when it comes his way. This theme of acceptance could definitely help the community as a whole as we consider the middle school climate.

BUDGET OF PROGRAM

For this program to work properly, books need to be given to the students with the understanding that they will pass them on to a friend, teacher, parent, or another as quickly as possible. The expectation is that there will be enough copies for all students, staff, and parents who would like to read the book to get the opportunity to read it. In order for that to work, we need to have 100 copies of the book that will get passed around by the students during the duration of the program and beyond. Since the books will not be catalogued or formally kept track of, I cannot use the book budget to purchase them. I plan to ask PTA to purchase the books for this initial year, but I will need additional funds for the author visit that I would like to plan as the culminating event for the program. Additionally, the library will host events to entice the students to continue reading the book throughout the school year. We will host events after school such as tie-dyeing shirts, friendship bracelet making, cupcake decorating, earthworm workshop and so on.

TIME FOR PROGRAM

To make this program successful, I will need to have the time to promote it among staff and students.

1. Time at a staff meeting to explain and promote the program.
2. Time with each student to be availed of during library orientation.
3. Time for promotions in the announcements.
4. Time for explanation on the release date.
5. Time for students to see the author. I would like to have all students hear the author speak, so I need the support for all classes to be brought to a central location.

6. Time at subsequent staff meetings to provide ways to use the novel in the classrooms, such as warm-ups, among others.

WRAP-UP

I know that a program like this is not cheap, and money is tight, but our students deserve the best from us. My experience has shown me that the number one way to get a student to read a book is for a friend to suggest it. Even students who are avid readers and who literally read one or two books a night want to read what their friends are reading. As evidenced throughout the novel *Schooled*, children want to fit in. Won't it be great to have something like a great novel being the way students are fitting in around here? Yes, I think so, too.

If you must provide a different type of meeting because of your audience, you will be promoting excitement as well as explaining the program. You will not need to discuss the specifics of the benefits to the program or the costs, as was mentioned above. You will just want everyone in the meeting to understand what you are doing and want to read the book for themselves. Here is an example of what was done at a staff meeting:

Good afternoon! I asked for a few minutes to tell you about something that is extremely exciting, and you all get to be a part of it. I have put 10 books in random staff mailboxes. I am asking you to read the book and pass it on to another staff member, who will then pass it on to yet another staff member until it has passed throughout the school. I have attached a page to the front page of the book so that you can sign the book before you pass it on to another person. This way, we can look back at the book to see the trail of readers. In the fall, on September 16, I will have two books for each advisory teacher to hand out to two random students in their advisory class. We will ask that student to read the book quickly and pass it on to another student, a teacher, or a parent, who will then pass it on, and so on.

[Note: You may want to have a copy of the following ready to give to staff as they leave the meeting.]

Capricorn Anderson has lived on a compound his entire life. He has been homeschooled, and he has had very little contact with the outside world until . . . chapter 1 . . .

I was thirteen the first time I saw a police officer up close. He was arresting me for driving without a license. At the time, I didn't even know what a license was. I wasn't too clear on what being arrested meant either.

But by then they were loading Rain onto a stretcher to rush her in for X-rays. So I barely noticed the handcuffs the officer slapped on my wrists.

"Who's the owner of this pickup?"

"It belongs to the community," I told him.

He made a note on a ring-bound pad. "What community? Golf club? Condo deal?"

"Garland Farm."

He frowned. "Never heard of that one."

Rain would have been pleased. That was the whole point of the community, to allow us to escape the money-hungry rat race of modern society. If people didn't know us, they couldn't find us, and we could live our lives in peace.

"It's an alternative farm commune," I explained.

The officer goggled at me. "Alternative, you mean like *hippies*?"

"Rain used to be one, back in the sixties. There were fourteen families at Garland then. Now it's just Rain and me." I tried to edge my way toward the nursing station. "I have to make sure she's okay."

He was unmoved. "Who is this Rain? According to her Social Security card, the patient's name is Rachel Esther Rosenblatt."

"Her name is Rain, and she's my grandmother," I said stiffly. "She fell out of a tree."

He stared at his notes. "What was a sixty-seven-year-old woman doing up a tree."

"Picking plums," I replied defensively. "She slipped."

"So you drove her here. At thirteen."

"I drive all the time," I informed him. "Rain taught me when I was eight."

Sweat appeared on his upper lip. "And you never thought of just dialing 911?"

I regarded him blankly. "What's nine-one-one?"

"The emergency number! On the telephone!"

I told him the truth. "I've talked on a telephone a couple of times. In town. But we don't have one."

He looked at me for what seemed like forever. "What's your name, son?"

"Cap. It's short for Capricorn."

He unlocked my handcuffs. I was un-arrested. (Korman 2007, pp. 3–5)

Cap is a very forthright character and extremely honest. Imagine what it would be like on his first day of middle school. Well, Rain is not doing too well, so that is exactly what happens. Cap gets to attend Claverage Middle School as an eighth grader. Here is what his first day is like:

"What are you looking at, jerkface?"

"What are you looking at, buttwipe?"

The first boy swung his book bag around and slammed it into the side of the other's head. He responded by punching the first boy in the nose, and soon the two were rolling on the grass, grunting and raining blows on one another.

I was horrified. I'd read about physical violence, but this was the first time I'd witnessed it in real life. It was sudden and lightning fast. Wild, vicious, ugly.

In seconds, a ring of spectators formed around the brawlers. Their gleeful chant echoed all around the schoolyard.

"Fight! Fight! Fight! Fight! . . ."

"Break it up!" A teacher burst into the circle, a brawny man with a whistle around his neck. He squeezed himself between the combatants and pushed them apart. "All right, who started it?"

"He did!" the two chorused, each pointing at his opponent.

The teacher gazed around at the spectators. "Any witnesses?" Nobody said a word. "Come on, who saw what happened?"

"I did," I volunteered.

"Well?"

"Buttwipe wanted to know what jerkface was looking at, and jerkface wanted to know what buttwipe was looking at." I turned earnest eyes on the bloody and dirt-smeared brawlers. "You were barely three inches apart. Couldn't you see you were both looking at each other?"

The teacher reddened. "Who do you think you are, Jerry Seinfeld?"

"You must have me confused with another student," I told him. "My name is Capricorn Anderson."

"Are you talking back to me?"

I hesitated. The whistle-teacher had asked me a question, and I'd answered by talking. "Yes?" I ventured uncertainly.

By the time he was finished yelling, both fighters had boarded their buses and gone home. I was the one who got sent to Mr. Kasigi's office.

I was waiting on the bench when Mrs. Donnelly appeared.

I leaped up. "Is Rain going to be okay?"

"That's why I'm here. Let's take a ride over there and find out." Her brow furrowed. "What are you doing in the hot seat?"

"I have a smart mouth," I replied honestly. "It's against the rules." (Korman 2007, pp. 18–20)

Cap attends public school for the first time in this book, but it is a great read about how everyone is schooled at Claverage Middle School. Don't miss out, *Schooled* by Gordon Korman.

Marquee, Screensaver Scrolls, and Displays

Inform your community of the upcoming RIF program and publicize the RIF title through press releases and public service announcements. Create small signs with stands that can be placed at the circulation desk. Build on the program over time by posting pictures or names of past participants in the library. Create a display with a copy of the book, photos of the author and participants, and other books by the author. If you have access to a display case, you can include some tangible objects that relate to the book's theme. For example, a friendship bracelet could be included for *Schooled*. Or, use your bulletin board to post photos and photocopies of the book cover.

Create mystery around the upcoming title or author with signage that states "What will the next book in the Read It Forward program be? The title will be announced on (date/time). Stay tuned for details!" You might even get creative and make a jigsaw puzzle out of the book cover, and add one piece a day to your sign, eventually unveiling the entire cover. The first person to guess the book gets a token prize.

Posters and banners can be created as well, and placed throughout the school or library. If you have enlisted the aid of the art teacher, it could be an assigned project in that class.

Marquees

If you have a marquee, you definitely want to use it to advertise the program. Below are two examples of what was done on one marquee:

Read It Forward Launch
Wednesday, September 16
For more details, check library wiki

and

Have you been Schooled?
Friendship Event
Thursday, October 15
@ Your Library

If you do not have ready access to the school marquee, you could have a running marquee on the school computers with similar messages. This could serve you well throughout the program if you change it often and the students get in the habit of looking for new messages on the screens.

SCREENSAVER SCROLLS

Screensaver scrolls are useful in getting the attention of students when they sit down at a computer in the library or the computer lab. They are simple to construct, but to be most effective, they need to be changed on a regular basis. Directions for adding a screensaver scroll.

1. Click on the Start menu at the bottom of the screen.
2. Click on Control Panel.
3. Choose Display from the list.
4. Click the Screensaver button.
5. Choose Marquee from the drop-down menu.
6. Click Settings.
7. Type the message that you would like to have scrolling across the screen.
8. Once you have typed your message, choose the speed. Then, click OK.
9. You may preview your message by clicking the preview button.
10. Once you are satisfied with the message, click Apply and OK.

The above directions are for Windows XP. If you have a different operating system, the specifics may vary slightly.

Displays

Create a mystery surrounding the possible title. An extremely effective way to get the students' attention is to set up a mysterious display. Some suggestions for this include the following:

1. You could have a large poster that you cover with a piece of black butcher paper. Strategically remove pieces of the butcher paper during the days leading up to the reveal date. For *Schooled,* you could reveal pieces of the peace sign or parts of a school bus.

2. You could put up signs around the library on bright yellow paper with different words that are meaningful to *Schooled* such as Tai Chi, Tie-Dye, Cap, Rain, Middle School, C Average, Halloween, Dance, Eighth Grade, President, and so on. One school even put them up every day for the week leading up to the reveal date. The clues got progressively easier as the date got closer. One thing to keep in mind is that if you do not want the students to figure it out too quickly, make sure that they will not be able to type the words into the online catalog to get the title of the book. One other tip is to put the date in the corner of the bright yellow signs so that the students can be reminded of the reveal date and connect the words to it.

3. You could put the reveal date on a cutout paper silhouette of a cap, perhaps a baseball cap. Cut them out and plaster them all over the school. It is a very subtle clue, but it is fun to hear their ideas of what the book could possibly be. One sixth grader was convinced that the title was *Caps for Sale.* I am sure that my leaving the online catalog on a page displaying that title had nothing to do with his wrong assumption.

Of course, not every librarian's personality will work with keeping a secret and creating the mystery, but it is *so* much fun if you can accomplish the task.

Exhibit Theme and Author's Other Titles

Another great way to promote extra reading is to display information about the author and other titles written by the author. Once students have read the RIF title, they will want to read more books by the same author. If you have a book that has a sequel, then you will be able to point them to the next title easily. If you choose a book whose author has written many titles, then you have plenty of options. Gordon Korman has written more than 40 titles, so we were able to have a healthy display of books on a wide variety of topics.

Additionally, you will want to have a display of books that are similar to the RIF book. Students will come in asking for something like the novel they just read. Some similar titles to *Schooled* are: *Zen and the Art of Faking It, Does My Head Look Big in This?, Poison Ivy, The Girls, Gifted, Inventing Elliot, Stargirl, Three Rotten Eggs, Racing the Past,* and *Hoot.* By having the list ahead of time, you will save much work and frustration as the program continues. Also, you will be promoting more reading, which will lead to more reading, which will lead to more reading. Awesome!

Post Pictures of Participants

If you have promoted well among the staff, you can use their pictures as a first picture display. You can use the ALA READ poster template. It is an easy template that is widely recognized. You could put their pictures in a long bus as passengers, or you could display smaller busses with the participants as drivers. Students love to see their pictures, so this could definitely heighten the excitement of the RIF program.

Post Names of Participants

Most of us chose to post the names of participants on a large display either of a peace sign or a bus. Some librarians were able to enlist help from the art teacher and the art students to design a super display. If you can get students to design the display, they will constantly be checking to see the names of the participants as it affects their art work. Additionally, they will want to have their names on the display as participants, and they will want their friends' names on the display as well. As seen below, students were asked to sign a bus that was then displayed around the large *Schooled* display.

Announcements

If you are in a school library, have PA announcements read by the librarian, students, teachers, parents, or administration. Have someone on your committee who is a good writer put together something clever and attention-grabbing, if you can. For example, on the reveal date, you will definitely need a clever announcement to get the students excited about reading the book.

Students: You will see packages all over school with caution tape on them. These are the RIF books. We encourage you to pick up the package, open it with care, and read it quickly. Then, we want you to pass it on to a friend who will then pass it on to a friend, who will then pass it on to a friend, and so on. Once you have read the book, go to the library and get a special, highly coveted Peace necklace. Only the coolest students will be wearing them this year.

Or, you could go with an announcement that involves an explanation of the book's plot:

Remember what your first day of middle school was like. You may have been thinking about seeing your friends, wondering if you would be in class with anyone you know from your elementary school. In *Schooled* by Gordon Korman, the main character Cap Anderson is entering eighth grade at Claverage Middle School. Cap has never been to a public school. In fact, Cap has not had much contact with anyone except his grandmother, Rain.

Will he survive? How will the other students treat him? Find out exactly who gets schooled in this year's RIF title *Schooled* by Gordon Korman.

If you find a book with caution tape around it in the hallway, feel free to take it, read it, and pass it on to a friend. Then, go to the library to add your name to the wall of all of the people who have been *schooled* this year and pick up your specially designed pencil.

Bookmarks and Incentives

Creating bookmarks and other incentives, such as pencils with "Have You Been Schooled?" written on them, peace necklaces, candy corn, notebooks with peace symbols, peace sign temporary tattoos, peace tie-dye stickers and other titles by Gordon Korman, will also help build awareness and spread the word about your program. Be creative or let other committee members or volunteers get in on the action. You may wish to ask your local bookstore to donate bookmarks; or a local business may be willing to donate small tokens that relate to your theme. For example, you could ask for tickets to a sporting event from a minor league team if your book is sports-related. If you book has food in the title, such as *Donut Days* by Lara Zielin, you could ask a donut shop to give coupons for a free donut. These are just two of the many ways that you can get items donated and involve your community in the program.

CLICKS—ELECTRONIC RESOURCES

Be sure to take advantage of electronic resources to promote your program. Post announcements on your library webpage, the school website, and in electronic newsletters. Send e-mails to students, and follow up with reminders. If you use social media—such as Facebook and Twitter—use them to announce the book and any programs or events you might have associated with it.

We developed a wiki where we put information for the students to see. We put pictures on the wiki so that students across the district could see what other students were doing. We also encouraged the students to post comments about the book and converse with each other about characters, motivations, and so on.

A wiki is a great way to quickly put information on the web for use in your school, district, state, or even throughout the world. When we mention our students having access to the internet, nervous tensions rise in some areas, but wikis can be set up with three levels of permission. The first level is public, which means that everyone can view and edit pages. The second level is protected. In this level, everyone can view pages on the wiki, but only members can edit the pages. The third level is private so that only members of the wiki can view and edit the pages. Additionally, you can choose whether or not to allow message posts from nonmembers.

We chose the protected level so that it could be visible to everyone, but we wanted to be able to monitor the content. Below is a screenshot of the home page for the wiki that was set up for our RIF project. You can get as creative as you want with the wiki design. You can even have students help you with the design. We chose something very simple because we were looking for ease rather than many bells and whistles.

There are many services where you can set up a wiki including Wikispaces or pbwiki. Setting up a wiki takes just a few minutes. Below are the instructions for setting up a wiki using Wikispaces.

Step 1 Join Wikispaces by creating a username and password. Once you join Wikispaces, you can set up a wiki.

Step 2 Choose a name for your wiki. We chose roundrockreaditforward as the title for our wiki.

Step 3 Choose which level of permission you would like for your wiki to be. You may need to consider what will fit into your electronic policies.

Step 4 Choose what type of wiki you are developing from the drop-down menu.

Now, you have a wiki. To design your wiki and to make it personal for you, go to http://help.wikispaces.com/Teacher+Help for answers to your design questions as well as how to set up accounts for students. An announcement for a wiki is shown below:

On Wednesday of this week, our library kicked off a special school-wide reading program called Read It Forward! The purpose of the program is to encourage all of our students to read and discuss the same book. One hundred copies of the book *Schooled* by Gordon Korman were anonymously dropped into lockers Wednesday morning. Inside of the book is a sticker with instructions for students to read the book, sign their name on the inside, and then pass it on to a friend or classmate. We hope that each book will be passed on at least five times prior to the author's visit on January 30. Students who read the book are encouraged to post their names on the Read It Forward! wall in the library and to participate in the other activities that will be tied to the book. Please check the library webpage for the school survey and other activities, including a link to a districtwide wiki where students may post their thoughts and comments about the book.

Finally, if your school or library has a closed circuit channel, consider airing a PowerPoint announcement on it, or some other recording such as a book talk, presentation, or book trailer.

FLICKS—MULTIMEDIA RESOURCES

Today, most libraries and schools have access to multimedia resources of some sort. Consider using Animoto or other web applications and software to create multimedia promotions for your program. For example, you (and your committee or volunteers) might create book trailers to show on your library's closed circuit channel, or post on YouTube or Vimeo. This can be as simple as recording a book talk as a podcast, or as complex as something acted out with costumes and props and recorded with a video camera. This is a perfect type of project for teens, so consider recruiting your Teen Advisory Board or Book Club to help.

PSA by Teen Advisory Board (TAB) or Book Club

Ask your TAB or book club to create a public service announcement (PSA) to be aired on a student broadcast. An example script for the PSA is shown below.

Hey, have you been schooled yet?

I'm wearing my awesome necklace, and you, too, could wear one by following 4 easy steps.

Step 1 Read the book.
Step 2 Sign the book.
Step 3 Pass the book on to a friend.
Step 4 Go to the library and complete the survey.

It would be fantastic if everyone could be wearing these when Gordon Korman comes to visit us in January. Don't be left out!

Video

One way to promote excitement is to develop a video to play for the students. Here is an example of a video with the sole purpose of surrounding this reading program in intrigue and mystery. If you do decide to create something with minors, be sure to get all needed releases and waivers prior to embarking on the project. You will also need to decide where you plan to place your video and you will have several choices: YouTube, TeacherTube, or embedding it. How to do this is shown below.

One librarian created the video and shared it with the other librarians. Some of the librarians were able to show the video to their patrons without having to create all pieces of the program from scratch. The video was created using Photostory. It was one way to promote excitement when it was played for the students. Here is an example of a video whose sole purpose was surrounding this reading program in intrigue and mystery.

Although one librarian created it, all nine of us used it in the weeks before the release date. For the first time, we knew that it was vital to the program's success to have the idea of something coming soon constantly playing on their minds. Since it is impossible to show a video in a book format, below are the steps taken to create the actual video used in the program.

1. Create slides in PowerPoint or Google slide presentation format.
2. Save slides as pictures in .jpg format.
3. Import these pictures into PhotoStory.
4. Make music with the tools in PhotoStory.
5. Save the video to computer.
6. Upload the video to YouTube. (Even though we shared resources through our school district, we felt it was important not to clog up the district's storage with multiple copies of the videos on the server. By uploading to YouTube, the video was available for all to use.)
7. Embed the video on webpage or wiki.

If you have not uploaded a video to YouTube, the instructions are below.

UPLOADING VIDEO TO YOUTUBE

1. You will need to set up an account with YouTube.
2. YouTube will send an e-mail to verify that the e-mail address given to them is valid. Click on the link in the e-mail.
3. Click on the button at the top titled upload.
4. For more information, you can read through the YouTube handbook.

You have created your video, and have uploaded it to YouTube; you may also want to load it onto TeacherTube. Instructions for doing that are shown below.

UPLOADING VIDEO TO TEACHERTUBE

1. If you do not have an account on TeacherTube, you will need to sign up for one.
2. Once you have your account, log in and click on the Upload Button.
3. Fill in the requested info: Title of the Video, a brief description, tags (tags are keywords that people will search with).
4. Select 1–3 channels that fit your video post. Once again, this helps people in searching.
5. Click Continue.
6. Click on the Browse button and locate your movie file.
7. Choose if you want the video to be public or private and click on Upload Video.
8. That's it! Once the video is loaded, TeacherTube will provide you with a URL address to send to people, so you can share your video.

How to Embed Video

Instructions for embedding a video are given below for Teacher-Tube and on WikiSpaces. One caution: **When embedding videos from YouTube and other sites, after the video is played, it suggests other videos to watch, which may or may not be appropriate for students.**

Find the embed code:

1. Go to the TeacherTube video you want to embed.
2. Scroll down the page until you see the code labeled Embeddable.
3. Highlight that code and press Ctrl C.
4. Paste the code into the widget using the steps above.

How to embed a Video on WikiSpaces

1. Open the page to Edit mode.
2. Click on the TV icon—Embed Widget.
3. Choose the Video option and click on the video source. Embedding a video allows it to be played from the wiki, but it is not loaded on the wiki, saving you file space.
4. Paste the Embed code for the video in the space provided.

Since videos were an effective means of communication and promotion with the students, we produced more videos for the program using animoto. Animoto videos are easy, and students love them. Instructions for this are given below.

CREATING A VIDEO USING ANIMOTO

Animoto is a great tool to use to create videos with awesome graphics. Animoto allows you the opportunity to create something that looks like it took hours, but only takes a few minutes of your time.

How to create an Animoto video

1. Create an Animoto account at http://animoto.com/.
2. Choose your video style. You will be allowed to create a 30-second video for free. Click to create the video.
3. Now, you will want to bring in your pictures. You may upload from your computer or select from their collection, or you may retrieve them from another site such as Picasa, Flickr, Facebook, etc. If possible, it makes the process easier if you have put all of your photos in one folder. If you have done that, Animoto will pull everything from the folder, so you only have to click one time instead of having to pull from multiple locations.
4. Once you have all of the pictures that you need for the video, you will want to put them in order. You do this by simply clicking and dragging them to the desired order.
5. If you would like to have a title or text between the images, you simply click the capital T button at the bottom of the screen. This will bring you to a prompt bar that will allow you to type in up to 22 characters.
6. Now, it is time to add the music. Animoto has a decent selection of music, so I suggest looking there. Or, you can upload a song from your computer. You will just need to make sure that the song is an mp3 format.
7. Once you have the music, click the Create Video button. It may take a few minutes to render the video, but you can exit or start another video project while the video is being created. You will receive an e-mail when the video is complete.

One awesome feature is that you can share the video with friends without taking up e-mail or server space. Animoto stores the videos, and you can easily view them with your students. You can also download them to DVDs if you are in a situation where internet connections are spotty or unavailable.

Proper promotion of any reading is vital to the success of the overall program. By using bricks, clicks, and flicks, you can easily get the word out there about RIF.

CLOSING

Successful RIF programs require plenty of excitement-building activities such as these so that when the books are distributed, the students are ready to get the reading started. Chapter 6 will delve into the specifics of programming ideas that will continue to promote participation within the RIF Program.

REFERENCES

Korman, Gordon. *Schooled*. New York: Hyperion for Children, 2007.

CHAPTER 5
Distribute Books

Now that you've spent a lot of time building excitement, it's time to distribute the books and unveil the title. Hopefully, students will be eagerly awaiting the books. However, depending on the overall school climate, the students may not be as excited as you would like them to be. If you notice that the only excited person is you, there are a few things you can try that might spark that interest for Read It Forward! (RIF).

First, you might approach one of the faculty members who read the book prior to the reveal date. Give them some cryptic messages to leak to the students prior to the reveal date. Students love to think they are in on the secret before their friends. Be careful not to give out too much information, because you don't want the teachers to reveal the title before you get the chance. One way to do this is to ask the teacher(s) to just give away a few keywords. For *Schooled*, some keywords that would have students guessing and actually appear in the first chapter are:

Cap
Arrested
Plum Tree
Rain

If the students have not yet read the book, they will be very interested in understanding how these clues fit together. If there is time, and the teacher is willing to go along with an anticipatory exercise, you or the teacher could have students make up quick stories using these four words. Then, when the title is revealed and students begin to read the book, they can compare their stories to what Korman wrote in *Schooled*.

For public librarians, the same tactic can be used with a different medium. For instance, during the days leading up to the reveal date, post the words on the library website or in a high traffic area. You could even have a contest to see if children could guess the title of the book. On the website, post a google.doc form that gives you the date and time of the entry. If you are posting the words in a high traffic area, simply place a box there with blank forms, and make sure that the form includes a space for date and time. You might ask participants to turn the completed forms in to a staff member, especially if you are concerned about the exact time and date. Make good use of the students' need to know secrets as a way to build that excitement. We have found this to be a useful tool.

Here is an example of a form for each of the short essay anticipatory contests:

Name:

Date:

Here are four words that appear in the Read It Forward! book:

Rain, Cap, Plum Tree, Arrested

Write a quick paragraph that includes all four of the words. The paragraph must fit on the bottom of this paper. We will award prizes in the following categories: Most Creative, Closest to the Book, Best Overall Paragraph.

Here is an example of a form to use for the Guess That Title anticipatory contest:

GUESS THAT TITLE

Name: _____

Date: _____

Can you guess the title of the Read It Forward book by looking at just a few words?

Rain   Plum Tree

Cap   Arrested

Your title guess: _____

Another option for building excitement is to create a wordle. A wordle is a word cloud that is created by putting a passage of text into a website. The visual is created based on the frequency of the words used in the passage, with the words used most often represented in larger type, and those used less often in smaller type. This word cloud can be created with the opening scene in *Schooled*, where Cap gets "unarrested," or with a passage from whatever book you decide to use. Look for a long passage with a good variety of provocative words. Then, offer students the opportunity to guess the title based on the word cloud. One website that creates this type of word clouds is www.wordle.net. This is an interesting way to visually represent the words in the text.

To be sure that your unveiling is successful, consider how the books will be prepared and distributed. The following suggestions can help add to the fun and keep the program running smoothly.

PREPARE THE BOOK

Instruction Labels

Place a label with RIF instructions on the back of or inside the front cover of the book so that students know what to do with the book when they have finished reading it.

READ IT FORWARD

Congratulations! You are about to read a fabulous book that is part of the Read it Forward program. After you read the book, sign the inside cover, and pass it on to a friend, classmate, parent, teacher, or any other person for them to read and enjoy. Also see Mrs. _____ or Mrs. _____ in the library to receive a special treat, sign our poster, and let them know what you thought of the book. Enjoy!

Sign

Just as students will be asked to sign the books before passing them on, the students will enjoy seeing the librarian's signature inside the cover. By signing the books yourself, you are, in fact, giving permission to those students who may feel very strange about writing in a book that does not belong to them. If the librarian can write in the book, then it must be okay. There are many ways to sign the books. You can pick one of your favorite parts of the book, and say something such as "I really loved the part at the end of the story when Cap . . . well, I don't want to ruin it for you. See me when you are done, and you can tell me whether or not you have guessed it. Please enjoy, sign and pass it on to a friend. Mrs. Kay."

Now, that is a lot to say in a message when you have 100 books to sign, but you can rest assured that the students who received a book with the above message were more likely to come in and talk to me about the book than those that had a shorter message. However, you know what your time commitments are, and you have to make that decision. Since there will be a lot of books to sign, finding a quick blurb to add is less daunting, but still personal. "Vote for Cap" and "Happy Reading" are good examples. Or, you could just add a peace symbol with your name.

It is also very important where you place that signature. The inside flap and the title page are great places to sign, as they are highly visible. If there are multiple pages before your signature, the student might not see it. I suggest writing your message on the very first page, so that it is evident that you are giving students permission to add their names to the list of readers.

Wrap

To add to the excitement, wrap the books before distributing them. Purchase wrapping paper that goes with the theme of the book or even consider enclosing them in brown paper lunch bags that have been decorated. For *Schooled*, some of the librarians decorated the bags with a stamp of a school bus or had a trusted group of students and volunteer parents decorate them with peace signs. Others wrapped books in crime scene tape or twine. Students will likely be even more excited about getting to open the books, as though they are receiving a present. Well, in fact, they are receiving a gift—one of the best gifts, a great book.

DISTRIBUTE THE BOOKS

Administrators

It is always a good idea to have administrators fully involved in the program. Give your principal or library administrator a copy of the book to read, sign, and pass on. Students and administrators, both will enjoy being able to talk to each other about the book; and knowing that the principals or library director has read the book gives the program even more validity in the eyes of the students. If it is possible, hand out these copies well before the reveal date, as administrators tend to be busy people and the initiative is most successful when the administration has read the book at the very beginning of the effort. This provides them with a talking point with the students and staff. If you have talked to them about your various programming ideas, use this opportunity to share the validity of having them join in the activities. One of your favorite sights will be seeing your principal talking with a student about a book they have both read.

Teachers and Staff Members

If there are enough copies of the book, give one to each teacher. Students get very excited about the book when a physical education or social studies teacher is reading it. If there aren't enough copies for each teacher, at least try to give one to each of your language arts teachers or department chairs. Try not to put extra pressure on your teachers. Tell them that if they don't have time to read it, just pass it on. Ask them not to tell students that they themselves do not have time to read the book. Our experience has shown us that because the students will be sharing their excitement about the books, many of your teachers will want to read it too. It's wonderful for students to be able to have a conversation about a book with an adult on campus, whether it is a teacher, custodian, or classroom aide.

When giving books to teachers, try to give them the books over the summer to promote their excitement before the school year starts. Without diluting the excitement of the official reveal date, you want to have others read the book prior to that date.

One way to keep the excitement going is to create excellent displays—which will be fully discussed in a later chapter—that show immediate growth. If the students see that many others have read the book, they will be motivated to obtain a book as quickly as possible, so that their names can be added to that display. If no one is on the display for 2–3 weeks, the students could get discouraged or even forget about their initial excitement.

Use the below page to attach to the front of the book for the faculty.

You have been specially chosen to be among the first recipients of a Read-It-Forward Book!

Please read it for fun, then pass it on to one of your colleagues— preferably in your department.
On the front page, there is a lined page where I would like you to write your name and the date you received the book. When you pass it on to a friend/colleague, ask him/her to do the same.
I hope you like it.

New Teachers and Faculty Members

A good way to build rapport with new teachers and faculty members is to give them a copy of the book during New Teacher Orientation. With all the school and district procedures they have to become familiar with, many of them will appreciate being part of a school-wide program and getting the opportunity to enjoy a good book. This helps them immediately feel a part of the school, and gives them something to share with the students early in the year. Many times, new teachers will be your best allies and supporters of this program. If you have an orientation period with the new staff members, it is fun to have them participate in a giveaway such as putting numbers under a chair. For example, hold a trivia contest based on various aspects of the book. For *Schooled*, you could ask a question about the 1960s. This is a particularly fun game if you have varying ages among your new staff members. Some will have memories of the 1960s while others were not even born by that decade.

Book Club and Student Advisory Group

Students who enjoy reading and participating in school programs should be among the first to receive a copy of the book. They are already library advocates and will be a big help in spreading the word (and adding to the excitement).

Other Students

At the designated release time, hide the books around the school in places where they can be easily found (i.e., by the drinking fountains, bathrooms, benches, hallways). Be sure to distribute them so that students in all grades will have a chance to find a book. Don't forget students who might be in the gym or a fine arts class.

One of the librarians in our district drops the books anonymously into lockers. The students find the package when they go to their lockers first thing in the morning. Another way to distribute the books is to have teachers distribute them. Choose a class period and write a number on the books before giving them to the teacher. The teacher then gives the book to the student who has the corresponding number on their roll sheet.

To make sure that the teachers do not forget to distribute the books, deliver them personally, and talk to teachers face to face. This may not be possible in every situation, but it is helpful if you can be there in person. In our middle schools, we have advisory class periods. Some of us were able to distribute books through advisory class periods. We have 48 advisory classes, and I gave two of the books to each teacher, along with two random numbers. I asked them to give the books to the students whose names corresponded on their class rolls with the random numbers that I gave them. Of course, not every student is ready to read the book at first. In those cases, ask the teachers to just take volunteers, or have the student who does not want to keep the book choose who will get it in the classroom.

It was important to me to make sure that the books went out at approximately the same time, so I asked other staff members who do not have advisory classes to help me deliver them. This way, we were able to distribute throughout the building in five minutes.

Consider giving copies to teachers to distribute to their reluctant readers. It is a wonderful way to get these students to see the library in a favorable light.

Once the books are in the teachers' hands, it is time to make the big announcement. Using the loud speaker or announcement channel that your school has available, briefly explain to the students that the reveal date for the RIF title has finally arrived. Then, you can give a brief book talk or show a video book talk to give more information about the actual title.

New Students

Hold back a few copies of the book to give to new students throughout the duration of the program. It helps them feel like they're a part of the school when they can become involved in the program right away.

REDISTRIBUTE THE BOOKS

It's inevitable that some of the books will return to the library, usually because a student forgets and puts it in the book drop. Be sure to pass these back out to keep the momentum going. Finding someone who wants to read the book is easy—whether you offer it to students before school in the busy library or take it to the cafeteria at lunchtime.

CLOSING

With careful planning and preparation, moving the books should take care of itself. The time is well spent as it adds to the excitement of the program. All that's needed now are some programming ideas to keep that excitement going!

CHAPTER 6
Programming Ideas

With Contributions from Kate DiPronio

The way to keep the momentum going for Read It Forward (RIF) is to have special programming that supports the book and its theme. It is vital that the programming is interesting to patrons and has a connection to the book. We were fortunate with *Schooled* that it was rich with connectivity to activities as well as our curriculum.

FRIENDSHIP THEME

Friendship is a major theme of this novel, so a wonderful and inexpensive program is making friendship bracelets. You can get fancy with specialty beads or you can keep it simple with embroidery floss. Even if you do not know how to make them, your patrons likely will. One of the most heartwarming moments for us was having a sixth-grade girl teach an eighth-grade girl how to make a friendship bracelet with a special technique. These girls would not likely have taken the opportunity to visit with one another and share with each other if it had not been for the RIF program.

Friendship bracelets are easy to make, even using just embroidery floss. This is a very low cost option. If you can get it donated, as we did, the cost for the bracelets is nothing.

If you have never made these floss bracelets before, go to the Making Friends website (makingfriends.com/jewelry/bracelet_klutz.

htm) for clear instructions. On this website, there are other choices for bracelets as well. The instructions are easy to follow, especially for older elementary to middle school level students. Particularly helpful is the list of supplies needed for the project.

Consider holding your event as an after school program, as we did—A Friendship Frenzy. Keep in mind at that these types of events take some time and the students will get hungry, so you may wish to have snacks on hand. You can even offer students the opportunity to make a friendship snack as well. In the back of the library, students were given a 10 ounce-cup and encouraged to mix and match the ingredients with the emphasis being placed on the metaphor between the ingredients and the school student body. Each piece is good on its own, but the combination was even better, and so on.

Here are the ingredients that we had available for the students to put together in the friendship snack.

M&Ms

Goldfish

Raisins

Fritos

Cheerios (We used Honey Nut Cheerios, but you need to be sure to let students know in case they have nut allergies)

Teddy Grahams

Craisins

Chocolate chips

Rice Chex (You could use different types because of the many choices available)

Pretzels

We had one container each of these ingredients, except for M&Ms. I knew they would be popular, so I purchased three large bags. The invitation for the Friendship Frenzy is given below.

Friendship Frenzy
Thursday, November 13
3:30 p.m.–4:30 p.m.
@ Your Library
Design friendship bracelets to share
with old friends and new

ENVIRONMENTAL PROGRAMS

Another great tie-in into *Schooled* that also correlates to the science curriculum is the environmental angle. At one of the middle schools, an environmental expert was asked to come in and teach the students about worm composting. She had a composting container where students could add items as well as check on the progress of the compost. If the composting was successful, the compost could be given or sold to library patrons or used in the school garden.

We worked with the Texas Commission on Environmental Quality for this project, but the United States Environmental Protection Agency has a great website that lists each state, with their corresponding environment agencies. This way you can go to your state's resources to find local options for you. This contact information is: http://www.epa.gov/epahome/state.htm.

"Green" Event

As mentioned previously, one of the major themes in the book we chose was being environmentally sound. We decided to offer programming that introduced and supported the green phenomenon that is popular with young adults.

One such program we had success with involved transforming old t-shirts into shopping bags. The great thing about this activity is that everyone walks away with something that is extremely useful. If you go to the grocery store and buy something that leaks into this shopping bag, you simply throw it into the washing machine.

For the t-shirt activity, have the students bring in a clean t-shirt. Any size is fine. Just so you can include everyone, you may want to see if you can get some school t-shirts to have on hand in case students forget to bring their own t-shirt.

Instructions for T-Shirt Bags:

1. Fold the t-shirt in half.
2. Cut off the sleeves and the neck to form the handles.
3. Turn the t-shirt inside out.
4. Sew the bottom of the shirt, which is what forms the bottom of the bag. (To make the bag last, you will want to have sewing machines to sew the bottom part of the shirt. However, if you do not have sewing machines, you can

sew with just a needle and thread, or you can just hot glue the bottom of the bag.)

5. Embellish with ribbon, buttons, and other materials.

A number of books are available that offer specific instructions for green activities for teens, such as Valerie Colston's *Teens Go Green* (Libraries Unlimited, 2012); Juliette Goggin and Stacy Sirk's book, *Junk Genius: Stylish Ways to Reinvent Everyday Objects*; and Emma Hardy's *Green Crafts for Children: 35 Step-by-Step Projects Using Natural, Recycled and Found Materials*.

TIME-PERIOD PROGRAMS

Our book was set in the 1960s, which was the time of many easily recognized trends, one of them being tie-dyed clothing. To use the theme of tie-dyeing, we used both clothing and food, in the form of cupcakes.

Tie-Dyed Clothing

Along with Cap's 1960s lifestyle in *Schooled*, he was, of course, an expert at tie-dye. This brought along with it a super programming idea—tie-dyeing. With a little investigation, we found ways to tie-dye t-shirts, headbands, and even cupcakes—with edible ingredients, of course.

Here is an example of the invitation and permission form sent with the students for the event.

AFTER-SCHOOL

SCHOOLED EVENT

JANUARY 22, 2009

3:30 P.M.–5:00 P.M.

RMS CAFETERIA

**TIE-DYE CLOTHING AND CUPCAKE
DECORATING CONTEST**

We will be tie-dyeing headbands that will be provided for you. The paint will be provided. If you would like to tie-dye a shirt or socks, or any other item, you must provide the articles of clothing to tie-dye.

In order to participate in this event, you must be available for the entire event. If you have extenuating circumstances, you must get prior approval from Mrs. Kay to come late or leave early.

If you are bringing an article of clothing to tie-dye, please have a parent/guardian sign at the bottom of the page and return to the library by Tuesday, January 20, 2009.

Since this event is after the school day, please arrange for transportation at 5:00 p.m.

Although it is not mandatory, it would be very helpful if you could RSVP for the event so that there are enough supplies for everyone who wants to attend.

_____ I will be attending the event, but I will not be bringing any item to tie-dye.

_____ I will be attending the event, and I will have _____ to tie-dye.

_____   _____

Student Signature   Parent Signature

We required that students bring in either t-shirts or socks to tie-dye. We also required that students bring a permission slip signed by a parent to attend the event. While speaking with some students a week before the event, they expressed that they were just going to tie-dye whatever clothing they were wearing that day. It is important to keep the relationships with all stakeholders healthy and keep the channels of communication open, so we required this permission slip. This way, we knew that the student had permission to tie-dye the article of clothing they had with them.

We offered a free option for those that did not have something to tie-dye or forgot their articles at home. Students were able to tie-dye headbands made from a queen-sized sheet. This sheet cost approximately $8 and made over 100 headbands. We had two kinds of tie-dying: the messy kind and the relatively tidy kind.

The messy kind of tie-dying with t-shirts is an awesome activity, but it does require a place where you can create and then clean up the mess. We used the school cafeteria and art rooms so that we could easily clean the floor and tables. Even being in one of these locations, we still had to set up the rooms for the event.

We covered the tables with newspapers. You could use butcher paper or plastic tablecloths, but we found that the newspapers were more absorbent. Additionally, we were able to use old newspapers instead of new butcher paper or tablecloths. Having enough newspaper to put under the tables helps keep the floors clean as well.

We purchased a kit that had the different dyes, squeeze bottles, washing ingredients, and so on. You can get this type of kit at a local craft store such as Michael's or Hobby Lobby, or you can order online from places such as Oriental Trading or Dharma Trading.

We purchased a large tie-dye group kit from Dharma Trading. We found that it had the needed items and there was very little extra that we did not use. However, you can also customize the kit, choosing what is most important to meet your needs. Their website is extremely instructive, and we found their staff personable and helpful: http://www.dharmatrading.com/tie-dye/.

You can also find links to videos to show how to dye with certain patterns. We showed the students how to tie-dye using the spiral pattern. This pattern gives the option for many colors and creativity.

For those of you who either do not have the space or the patience for the messy tie-dyeing project, there is a great solution. For mess-free tie-dye headbands, you simply use markers and color on the fabric. Then, spritz rubbing alcohol on the colored designs. It will run slightly and give the tie-dye look.

With this approach, it was much easier to control the artwork; but for those students who did not feel comfortable drawing, it was a bit daunting. However, most of them enjoyed getting the opportunity to tie-dye and were good natured about it. The only problem that we had was the markers running out of ink. Be sure to stress to the students that in order to get the tie-dye look, they should not completely color in the fabric.

Tie-Dye Cupcakes

As we were discussing ideas for student programs, we considered ways to integrate food into our program, and came up with the idea of having the students make tie-dye cupcakes as a program or in conjunction with other tie-dye items.

Through some testing, I found three different ways to have fun with tie-dye cupcakes. Any of the three ways will work; you just have to decide what you have time to do.

Option 1

Materials Needed:

> 1 white or yellow cake mix and ingredients needed to cook cupcakes listed on back of box
>
> 4 different colors of food coloring
>
> 24 cupcake liners
>
> 1 container of white frosting

Prepare white or yellow cake mix as instructed on the package. Measure out 4½ cups of batter and put the ½ cup of batter into four separate bowls. Add red, blue, green, or yellow food coloring into each of the separate bowls. Layer the different colored batter into cupcake liners to ⅔ full. Each cupcake will be slightly different as you will layer them differently. We iced them with plain white icing since we wanted the color to show. You could also just use a plain glaze.

Option 2

Supplies Needed:

> Prepared cupcakes, enough for at least two per student
>
> Prepared vanilla frosting, enough to frost the number of cupcakes you have purchased
>
> A few tubes of different colored gel frosting

Prepare and bake the cupcakes. FunFetti cupcakes are a fun choice as there are colored candies in the mix. I asked volunteers to bring in premade cupcakes, which helped with my time and pocketbook.

Once you have the cupcakes ready, allow the students to frost the cupcake with vanilla frosting. Use the gel frosting to swirl the colors around to "tie-dye" the top of the cupcake. If you have time, it is fun to have a competition for the best tie-dyed cupcake. If you choose to have the competition, have extra cupcakes ready for the students to frost and eat while the competition cupcakes are being judged and votes are tallied.

Option 3

Supplies Needed:

> Cupcakes, at least one cupcake per participant
> White icing, enough to cover the number of cupcakes you will bake
> A few tubes of gel icing in various colors

Give each student a prepared cupcake. Take a corer, small scoop, or spoon and scoop out about an inch well in the middle of the cupcake. Layer the gel icing into the well until it comes up to the top of the cupcake. Ice the cupcake with the white icing. This cupcake will appear to be a plain cupcake but the tie-dye is in the middle. This approach allows for the possibility of an interesting conversation with the students. Cap was a person who was definitely more than he appeared to be on the surface. As you enjoy the cupcakes with the students, ask them about an instance in the book where one of the characters realized that Cap was different from what he originally appeared to be.

The possibilities for programs are truly endless with this book. All of us have specific strengths from which we can pull in order to make the books come alive for the students. Trying to conduct all of the programs listed here could be exhausting, so choose one or two that you can do well. This will make the RIF successful for a larger number of students. When I talk with students about what they like best about RIF, without fail, they list one of the special programs. Students love to get together with their classmates, and their parents love for them to get together with their friends to work on something meaningful. RIF programs provide that for the students and their parents.

These are some of the ideas that we had for *Schooled*. You can find more in titles such as *Teen Programs with Punch* by Valerie Ott; *Travel the Globe* by Desiree Webber et al.; *Story Celebrations* by Jan Irving; and *Library Programs for Teens: Mystery Theater* by Karen Siwak.

CLOSING

Once you have offered the book and the programming for the RIF book, it is time to decide how to end it meaningfully so that the participants feel some sense of accomplishment as well as anticipation about the next book.

CHAPTER 7
Keeping Track

With Contributions from Laura Stiles

Keeping track of successes and failures has never been more important in the library world than it is now. Between the increase in statistical accountability due to No Child Left Behind, standardized testing, and the economic downturn, librarians need to prove that the programs money is spent upon are successful. If a program is not successful, having statistical information to evaluate assists in improving the program or, if need be, in eliminating the program all together.

During our first Read It Forward (RIF) program, most of the nine Round Rock Independent School District middle school librarians kept track of student and faculty and staff participation in different ways, and kept track of other issues as well. Having learned from our first program, we have suggestions for compiling statistical information that will help you ascertain the success of your own program, and these can be used to encourage positive and continued support for your program once it's over.

The first is to use one of the various ways to check on whether the book was read. Some in our group used a simple quiz to see if students had read and comprehended the book. A more informal approach involves asking students about their favorite part, and then engaging them in a dialog with either the librarian or the library assistant. One librarian used an online survey through SurveyMonkey at www.surveymonkey.com.

Once you have determined that participants have completed the book, you can encourage them to sign their names on a paper bus cutout or any other meaningful object, such as a peace sign. The busses can be displayed in a prominent place in the library or right outside of the library. These displays serve as a reminder and will keep everyone excited about the program. Some students may even decorate their individual buses so that they can show their friends later.

As you arrange for program tracking, consider entering each participant's name into an Excel file or other spreadsheet as you receive their signed bus. I entered the participants' first and last names and grade level; in hindsight, I wish I had also kept track of their gender, as it would have been an interesting statistic to review later. A large portion of the students at my school have names that do not designate a gender, and so, going back to define gender would have been exceedingly time-consuming.

Having a spreadsheet that includes all of your RIF participants is valuable in several ways. First and foremost, it enables you to determine, at a moment's glance, how many participants you have. Additionally, it allows you to include all who have read the book in invitations to programming events. Finally, after your program is over, you will be able to easily identify your total number of participants by gender and grade level, or by whatever other information you have chosen to collect.

One technology-rich method of keeping track of the number of your RIF readers is to offer an online survey. Several websites can help you create your own survey. The service used most often by our librarians is www.surveymonkey.com. You must join this service to use it, but there is no cost to arrange a survey with up to 10 questions and up to 100 respondents. You can use one of 15 preset themes.

In creating your survey, consider how much information you would like to compile. While it seems intuitive to ask a wide variety of questions, sometimes the answers are not useful statistically, and additional questions can end up costing you. Therefore, choose your questions carefully.

Some questions that will provide good statistical information include:

Reader Designation: Are you a student or a staff member?

Are you male or female?

Are you a sixth, seventh, or eighth grader?

Decision to Read: What made you decide to read the book?

    a) my friends were reading it

    b) I heard about it on the school news and wanted to be part of the program

    c) I found a copy of the book and just decided to read it

Source of the Book: Did you:

    a) read a Read It Forward copy of the book?

    b) check the book out of the school library?

    c) check the book out of the public library?

    d) buy your own copy of the book?

Other questions that can provide you with valid information, even though the information may not be useful statistically, include:

Enjoyment: How would you rate the book?

    a) excellent

    b) acceptable

    c) not enjoyable

Are you interested in reading another book by the same author?

    a) yes

    b) no

In addition to these methods, one informal way to keep track of the books is having students sign the inside cover. It is important that students feel as though they were a part of the big picture; but not all students want to complete a survey, no matter how painless you attempt to make it. We, of course, offered rewards for completing the survey, but again, for some students, that was not enough of an incentive.

Rather than feeling defeated by the students' lack of initiative for completing the survey or providing feedback, consider simply letting them sign the books, so that anyone who gets the book knows who has read the book before them. Of course, there is no way to get statistics or quantitative feedback from that type of declaration from the students, but one of the most positive components of this particular program is that the students share with each other.

Ultimately, there is a fine line for keeping track of students reading the books. Of course, you want to obtain statistics so that you can show how many students are being impacted by the program and justify it to administrators and parents, but that cannot be the main focus of the program. You can assume that even if you have many students who will complete the forms, there will be some students who will not comply. If the students read the book, then that is the real focus of the program. In other words, try not to get caught up in the statistics. Put the books out for the students, encourage them to read quickly, pass it on to their friends and let you know about it. No matter how many students you hear from personally, those you do hear from will make it worth your time.

When you gather the statistics, be sure that you share them with your stakeholders through your library website, newsletter, and notices to parents. These avenues of communication are extremely important for your library program. Additionally, contact the local media so they can cover your library's efforts to promote literacy among all of your patrons. Whether you have charts through great statistics or you have touching anecdotes, make sure that you share the great things you are doing in your library through the RIF program.

CHAPTER 8
Culminating Event

With Contributions from Lori Lockwood

Although we have given you plenty of ideas of programs to keep the interest going in passing the book from person to person, it is important that the program has an ending time. To optimize complete success, be sure to establish an overall timeline with an ending date and a well-publicized culminating event. If your final event is attractive enough, students will take the extra time to complete the questionnaire form so that you have a record of their having read it.

CULMINATING ACTIVITIES

School size and budget are the two most important considerations when planning a Read It Forward (RIF) culminating event. In addition, the library's ability to access and use facilities should be considered. Planning your grand finale well in advance and having the support of the administration in the planning and programming will ensure success.

Cost guide:	
$$$$	$500+
$$$	$100–$499
$$	$50–$99
$	$49 and under

That being said, there are many types of events you can organize to celebrate your program. What follows are a few types of events we have found successful.

Author Visit ($$$$)

An author visit requires a healthy budget and advanced planning. Many times, it may take a year or longer to book the author of your book. If one school or library cannot afford the honorarium, consider sharing a day with another school or public library. Most authors will split one day between two locations. In addition, a local bookstore or the publisher may be able to supply books for students to buy and have signed after or before the presentation. The library can also showcase the author's other works throughout the year, and if space is limited for the presentation, library staff can limit the attending students to those who have read the RIF selection or another of the author's works. A good guide for planning an author visit is Chapple Langemack's *Author Event Primer,* Libraries Unlimited, 2007.

School Dance ($$–$$$)

Life sometimes imitates fiction. At the conclusion of *Schooled*, the students plan a dance. At the end of the RIF, your school can hold a dance where everyone is dressed as one of the characters in the book, such as Capricorn. If you and your staff members choose to do a tie-dye activity as part of your RIF programs, students will have a readymade wardrobe.

Decorations for this type of dance are easy: peace signs and flowers made from colored butcher paper. Several party suppliers, on-line and storefront, have 1960s party kits with decorations and giveaways for the event. Place large pieces of butcher paper on the walls for students to sign. Recruit a D.J., and have him or her focus on 1960s music to complete the hippie theme. Tie-dyed sheets work well for tablecloths. Brave librarians can serve hummus and other vegan/vegetarian snacks for the students to try. If planning a dance at school is a logistical nightmare, the local branch of the city or town library may be willing to take on the task—another reason why collaborating with the local library is a good idea.

The dance could also turn into a fundraiser for the next year's program, or for bringing in the author. Give students who have completed the questionnaire form free admission, and charge admission for those who did not read the book and complete the form. Another alternative is to offer free admission for everyone and a free snack for the students who participated in the program, and charge other students for the food items. Our schools have successful money-making dances several times a year.

Book Party ($–$$)

For librarians who do not have the time, resources, facilities, budget, or support necessary to pull off an entire school dance, a smaller-scale celebration can be just as effective. If your library cannot schedule an event during the day by opening specific time slots to each grade level, an after-school event will also work. Librarians who do not have time to cover each of the programming ideas discussed in chapter 6 may choose to do them at the book party. Tables can be set up for crafts and games that relate to the book. For example, with our *Schooled* party, we set up nonelectronic games and tie-dyeing stations. Refreshments and music can also include items that related to the book. For *Schooled*, we offered vegetarian fare, and music included Rain's favorite group, the Beatles.

Read-In (Free–$$)

Offer students who have filled out a questionnaire at the completion of the book an invitation to an all-day Read-in at the library. You can set up small areas with bean bags, large pillows, or chairs for students' comfort, where students can spend time quietly reading a book of their choosing. Those librarians who allow occasional events with food may want to supply snacks such as cookies or pretzels and drinks, bottled water, hot chocolate. You may even tell the students they are allowed to come to the Read-in with their own pillows. The invitation and the book to read are the students' tickets into the event. Circulating a list of invitees beforehand to staff members allows teachers to decide who needs to stay and who can be allowed to miss a day of class, and librarians can decide if they want the event to be open all day for each student or to limit each student's time at the event. This event could also be held before or after school—if the library staff and volunteers can manage the extra time.

The major advantage to this event is the opportunity for offering a *very* cool event for free. Additionally, this event could tie in well to the theme of your book, depending on which book you choose. Instead of a sit-in in protest to some injustice, offer a read-in, where the students can relax and be rewarded for reading an awesome book. You might just start a revolution!

CLOSING

Although, as librarians, we are promoting reading for a lifetime, there needs to be a clear conclusion to your organized RIF program so that you can be ready for the next RIF book. If you go on too long, rather than offering more opportunities to read the book, the students will lose interest. Offer the culminating event while the students are still excited about the book, so that they will continue RIF for a lifetime.

CHAPTER 9
Year Two

After having such a great Read It Forward (RIF) program the first year, we decided that we wanted to pursue a second year for our students; and my hope is that you will choose to continue your RIF program, too. The process in the second year is a little different than when starting out, and we learned some further lessons; so I will show you how we worked through the steps for the next two years as well as what we are in the process of preparing for the next school year.

CHOOSE A GREAT BOOK

The book we chose in our second year was a mystery and adventure book entitled *I,Q Independence Hall* by Roland Smith. The two protagonists—one male and the other female—would speak to all of our students. The story is a quick-paced page turner. Although we did not specifically set out to choose a book in a different genre, we were hoping that we would find a title to appeal to even more of our patrons. In the following paragraphs, you will see how we went through a similar process in choosing this title as we did when choosing *Schooled*.

Again, this book was on the Texas Lone Star list, and the author of the book is prolific, with more than 30 titles attributed to him. *I,Q Independence Hall* is the first book in the series, and the thought of getting students excited about a series was definitely appealing. If the students are hooked with the RIF book, they will be looking for other books. When the author has written multiple books, have other titles by the author that you can offer the students. You can put up a display of his books, so they are all in the same place.

After talking through the possible programs and how it would work with the various classes in our school curriculum, our choices were determined. The specifics are explored in the following pages following our successful model from the first year.

OBTAIN BUY-IN

Once you have implemented the program the first year, you'll likely find it a lot easier to garner support for the program in the second year. If you have the opportunity, have a student present a copy of the book to a school board member and ask that school board member pass it on to someone, who would pass it on to someone else. This is a great bridge, and shows the board member how powerful your program is. As mentioned in chapter 2, getting the principal or library director to read the book and pass it on is essential to the success of your program. Additionally, giving a copy to your school superintendent or a library trustee can be a way to help your program grow in size. In other words, make extending beyond your building and immediate contacts a definite goal of your program.

Students share what they are excited about, so be sure to give them the opportunity to share with more than just other students. It would be awesome to have a student present the book to the superintendent and ask the superintendent to attend one of your programs. As a programming idea for I,Q Independence Hall—one of which includes a playoff of Guitar Hero/Band Hero/RockBand—one idea we came up with was to have the superintendent join one of the student bands in the competition. What a photo op!!!

As stated before, for both school and public librarians, it is essential to have buy-in from the staff. Don't forget to pass out copies for teachers to read over the summer. By doing this, they have time to enjoy it instead of adding to their overloaded plate at the beginning of the school year. You cannot take for granted that everyone remembers the program or its successes, but it is always a good idea to approach a new teacher on the campus with the book. This gesture will build a bridge for that new teacher.

For public libraries, a great way to get the word out for your program is to use the schools and home-schooling network in your communities. If you can work in concert with each other; everyone wins.

OBTAIN COPIES OF THE BOOK

Our first year of RIF was introduced in a program for school librarians at a meeting of the Texas Library Association, which led other school districts to participate in the program in our second year. While this was great for Texas children, it nearly sunk our program because we could not use our first option of obtaining the books—going straight to the publisher. Following the steps in chapter 3, we went straight to the publisher for this RIF program because these other school districts in Texas were joining us by using *I,Q Independence Hall*. They obtained copies through Scholastic before we did, and completely cleared out the warehouse for that school year. The publisher was able to give us a discount since we had booked Roland for an author visit at some of our schools. For many publishers, they will offer a discount as part of an author visit. This was a great lesson for us to make sure that we get the books early so that the price we had budgeted was indeed the price we paid.

PROMOTE EXCITEMENT

Even though you may have promoted the RIF program the previous school year, it is vital that you spend time promoting it in the same ways again. The face-to-face presentations are essential to the success of the overall program. Students actually like to hear from their librarian what the book is going to be, but if you make them wait to find out the title by just giving clues, you will build anticipation.

Another option is to book talk the book, so that they already know the title and a little about the plot before the reveal date. One of the librarians on our team created a video using Animoto that gave more of a hint of the book without giving away the title. This librarian shared the video with us through the Animoto site so that we could show the video to students through library orientation sessions. An anticipation video used during library orientation in the fall gives you face time with each student on campus.

Our displays for *I,Q* centered around music since that is a strong theme of the book. Some librarians used inflatable guitars and had the students put their names on guitar picks. I found a shower curtain that depicted a concert scene and created silhouette heads for participants to put names and add to the concert. The silhouettes were found in Microsoft clip art and cropped, so that we worked with only the heads of the bodies. The silhouettes were a nice touch, but it was labor intensive. Each silhouette had to be cut by hand. If you have student aides or any volunteers, ask them to do this sort of task for you; but if you have few volunteers, consider other ways to decorate. Another idea we had was to hang a large U.S. map on the wall, and have paper cutouts of guitars for the students to complete by adding their names and add to the map. Any of these ideas can work, depending on your situation. Just consider your space limitations, and find what would most excite your patron base. Because my library has a very large wall, I am always looking for something large to fill, so a shower curtain worked nicely. Another librarian only has the space of one bulletin board, so she had to choose the guitars and guitar picks.

Incentives are fun to create. In our second year RIF program, we decided to give away customized guitar picks with the *I,Q* logo. After gaining the publisher's permission, we used the logo on the cover of the book and put it on guitar picks. We worked with one of our vendors, RockSports, to get the logo printed on the guitar picks. Then, when students completed their survey and answered questions about the book, we gave them the guitar pick. If the student wanted to wear it as a necklace, we had a hole punched in the dot of the "I" in *I,Q*. Not every hole punch worked for us. The larger ones broke the pick. So, if you decide to do this, make sure that the hole is small enough before purchasing.

This incentive was not as popular as the peace necklaces were from *Schooled*. We also made the mistake of putting the year on the guitar picks. If you put the year on your incentive, you are stuck with using them during that year. In fact, I had ordered extra picks so that we could get a cheaper unit price. In fact, we have joked about using them for some type of recycling craft in the future. A commercial of a craft guru joked about using old credit cards to tile a swimming pool; I'm not sure that enough remain to tile our Olympic-sized swimming pool, but we definitely have enough for a fun kiddie-sized pool. In retrospect, a more conservative number should have been purchased, and definitely without the year printed on them.

DISTRIBUTE BOOKS

After learning about the previous distribution from *Schooled*, some of us changed while others distributed in the same way. Due to a complete school schedule change, I had the opportunity to distribute the books in a much different way. In the previous year, books were distributed in September on one of our early release days during our advisory time, so that one of the schools could begin programming right away. It sounded like a great idea again, so we decided to repeat the date; however, our school had a pep rally scheduled for that day, which changed the entire day's schedule. On pep rally days, there is no advisory time.

Of course, the logical distribution time was during the pep rally. At the beginning of the pep rally, I was announced and walked out to the music accompaniment of the James Bond theme. I explained about the release of the RIF title, and revealed that I would be dispensing the novels as soon as the students watched a book trailer about the title. It was fortunate that there were quite a few pre-made choices on YouTube, so one of those was used. A long time ago, I learned to save myself much-needed time by searching through YouTube to see if there is a viable book trailer option.

The names of the students, randomly chosen, were announced and they were each given the book with the charge to read it quickly and pass it on to a friend. Additionally, random copies were placed around the school a week later, and then, again, a week later. This helped to keep the interest in reading the book alive. I felt it was important that students saw me with my stash of books that I was placing in the hallways, so I distributed these during times when students would also be in the hallways.

The books were signed in a similar fashion as they were with the *Schooled* books. The messages included "What is your favorite part?" "Enjoy reading!" "Will Q figure it out in time?" Since the book has black pages, a silver Sharpie was used, but it was not possible to write a long message. With these books, there was not as much signage as with the *Schooled* books. In order to get thoughtful responses from the students, it seemed best to have a thoughtful remark with my signature.

PROGRAMMING

Although the programming was not quite as obvious with the various themes in *Schooled*, we were able to devise several different extracurricular events that engaged the students in the novel. The curricular programs begin with geography.

For the geography program, one of the librarians developed a "Where in the U.S. is Q?" Then students could figure out answers to the geography questions and map them out.

Another program possibility is to let the students use Google Earth to see where Q and Andrea went on their journey across the United States. It takes a little more time, but if you can set up locations and put in facts for participants to read about the locations, it is a good assignment for your students to help you set up the facts for themselves. Students love looking at destinations using Google Earth. It is a great tool that can work to promote this book as well as give students skills for the future.

Since the parents in the book are rock stars, having this music program connection is a natural fit. This can take on in many formats; you just need to consider what is going to work best for you and your students. For example, you could host a lip sync contest, a talent show, an American Idol competition, or you could use a gaming device and host a Rock Band or Band Hero competition. Originally, we had hoped to have a districtwide concert where each school presented 1–2 acts per school, but this had to be put aside due to logistical problems.

Our backup to the districtwide concert became holding a video game competition. The hope was that the competition would be across the district, but the video capabilities were limited. In retrospect, the program could have been students at two schools competing against each other, but that wasn't suggested until the individual competitions were over. However, the individual competitions were a complete success, and very popular with students, so this approach is highly recommended.

Since the program sets the points, scoring is easy. One librarian had two groups as finalists in the school competition—one novice and one expert. The expert group thought they would be able to beat the novice group easily, but the novice group worked with a song they knew and were realistic with their skills. In the end, the novice group scored higher, thereby winning the competition. With my school, we started our efforts by advertising this program, and made sure students knew that this was an invitation-only event. They were also told that they could only receive an invitation if they completed the form online for reading the RIF book. Many students had read the book and passed it on to a friend, but did not complete the online form until they heard about the Band

Hero/Guitar Hero competition. Suddenly, there was an onslaught to complete the forms. As cliché as it sounds, we had a rockin' good time!

Another program suggestion we had for this book was to host a magic program. This program was not chosen by any of the librarians, but it is a definite avenue to take with this novel. Q is constantly performing card tricks. If you can find a magician, that would make for a great program. You could also schedule an afternoon of magic, where students brought their own magic tricks. Book the cafeteria if your group is too large for the library. Have students sign up and perform for their fellow students. To produce the right atmosphere, host a Read-A-Latte afternoon, where you sell cups of hot chocolate or cappuccino for $1 per cup and have the magicians roam through the tables performing, much like you would find in an outdoor café. This would be fun for everyone, and the students will have subsidized the activity by purchasing the drinks.

Of course, the purpose of the RIF program is to promote reading, but sometimes, a great way to get students to read a book is to show them the movie counterpart. This book reminded me of the movie, *National Treasure* due to the fact that it considered various U.S. historical places and situations. After discussion with the other middle school librarians, it was quickly apparent that my choice was similar to others who had made the same connection.

If you show a movie with more than 25 students, you will need to get a license to show a movie for entertainment, but you can do this easily. Use Movie Licensing USA, www.movlic.com. You can either buy licensing for one movie or for an entire year. If you approach your principal or PTA, you might be able to get funding for the year so that they can host their movie nights as well.

KEEPING TRACK

As in the first year, students were asked to sign the books before they passed it on to the next student. This method is not ideal, but it still seems to be the preferred method. However, since we do not see the books, it is very hard to show any statistics, so we continue to search for other methods.

We learned from the previous year that an online tracking method worked well for us. For *Schooled*, one of the librarians used

SurveyMonkey; but in the second year, for *I,Q,* we decided to use Google Docs so that we could have unlimited users. This worked well, and it offered the students an opportunity to see the statistics for the different schools. Instead of each school having its own separate form, we designed a single form for Google Docs, so that everyone could use the same one. Each of our librarians put a link on his or her respective pages, and when the students completed the form, the answers were automatically set up in a spreadsheet. Additionally, for the questions that had set answers, circle graphs were completed, so we had instantaneous statistics to show how many students had completed the form. You can go to the following web address to see the live form. https://spreadsheets.google.com/spreadsheet/viewform?hl=en_US&formkey=dG1pM21xRm9WZGg0WFdYZHE0a3lFTnc6MA#gid=0.

RIF: I, Q: INDEPENDENCE HALL

Please complete the following questions. You must complete all questions to be eligible for prizes and RIF programming.

* = Required

Last Name *_____

What is your school affiliation? *_____

Grade Level *_____

Language Arts Teacher * If you are a faculty or staff member, please

type in NONE. _____

Who is the author? *

- O   J.K. Rowling
- O   Stephenie Meyer
- O   Rick Riordan
- O   Roland Smith
- O   Gordon Korman

Would you recommend the book? Why or why not? *

```

```

What surprised you most about the book? *

```

```

Rate the book. *

O   Fantastic, where is the sequel?
O   Great!
O   It was okay
O   Did not like it

CULMINATING EVENT ACTIVITIES

Many of the programming ideas mentioned on the previous pages will also work as culminating events. Most of us used the video game competition as our culminating activity.

Some of us were able to bring in the author as well. However, author visits are expensive, and after having the author from the previous RIF program the year before, some of the schools could not afford to bring him in to speak. Those of us who brought him in decided that we would like to have him come at the beginning of the program rather than at the end. Therefore, we could not consider the author visit as a culminating event but used it as an excitement builder.

CLOSING

The video game playoff was a great way to end our RIF program because it offered an interactive approach, which students really loved. Not only did we promote reading through our awesome RIF program, but we promoted the library in general by offering such a fun program. Plus, now they knew that I had some mad singing skills in Band Hero.

CHAPTER 10
Year Three

With Contributions from Lori Loranger

If a program is going to have lasting power, you need to be committed to it for a certain time period. Of course, it is essential to be honest with what worked and what did not work. Our first year with Read It Forward (RIF) was superb and our second year was very good. Then, we hit a few snags. To fully understand what happened, you have to refer to the data. At the end of the chapter, you will find an analysis of another librarian in the district. But, let's review the narrative of how this happened.

The process is laid out in this chapter. The process we had established was a good one, but for some reason, in the third year, we did not follow some of our own advice. Year 3 was not as successful for us, and we are offering you the benefit of learning from our mistakes during this year. The steps followed are the same as those for the first two years.

CHOOSE A GREAT BOOK

The book we chose in our third year was a ghost story entitled *The Hunt for the Seventh* by Christine Morton-Shaw. Again, the two protagonists are a boy and a girl, this time, a brother and sister. We figured this would still speak to all of our students. The story seemed to be a quick-paced page turner. The book chosen was on the Texas Lone Star list again, but the author has not written many books. Additionally, we did not plan the author visit as a part of the program because the author was not available for that. At first, this did not seem to be a problem, but a precedent had been set, so the students and the staff asked repeatedly when the author was going to come to campus. In retrospect, we could have explored other options, such as a Skype visit, a Google hangout, or a live chat, but we didn't think of that.

Before we made our final decision on the book, we discussed the various curricular connections. Even though the focus was on pleasure reading, we knew it had to work with the various classes in our school curriculum in order to get the essential buy-in. The specifics are explored next.

OBTAIN BUY-IN

Because the program had been implemented the first two years, it was easier to get continued support. As was mentioned in chapters 2 and 9, getting the principal to read the book well before the launch date is essential to the success of the program. If you take the extra time to get other administrators and the school board involved, it definitely pays off. With our current economic climate, this is a great way to highlight the impact libraries have on literacy for all.

It remains essential to have staff members read the book before your launch date as well. Don't forget to pass out copies for teachers to read over the summer.

OBTAIN COPIES OF THE BOOK

In our third year, we were able to get many of the copies of the book from Scholastic, and use some of our Scholastic dollars. It is great to use the dollars if you can so that you can save money for other aspects of the program. We could not get enough copies from Scholastic, so we went through Barnes and Noble to supplement. Again, they gave us a discount, and we were able to get the books quickly. They offered us a 20 percent discount.

PROMOTE EXCITEMENT

As in previous years, we talked to students, either face-to-face or through book talks. Again, I showed an anticipation video during the library orientation so that I had face time with each student on campus.

Placing these slides into a PhotoStory presentation with some creepy music gave a small clue to the book. Additionally, the color scheme anticipation video was black, yellow, and reddish/orange—the same as the cover of the book. No student in my library has guessed the title based on that, but in the future, they may figure it out from the preview.

The displays for *The Hunt for the Seventh* revolved around a forest and garden theme, and, of course, the number seven. One librarian found a great forest scene at a party store in our city. It was not large enough for our library wall, but we had students work on the display. They put two of the pieces together so that it gave the wall a 3D effect. Then, the participants put their names on the number 7 die cuts. If you do this type of thing, select a color that blends in with the background as a play on the title. We had a cool background; but in retrospect, it might also have been fun to have the 7s really stand out so they weren't too obscure for students,

Our incentives were an easy one for this year, silly bandz. Silly bandz are just rubber bands in fun shapes such as puzzle pieces, animals, hearts, or sports shapes that were a popular item for students to wear. Students wore multiple silly bands on their wrists, sharing the different shapes all over campus. To capture that excitement, many different types were purchased, including numbers. Our vendor was the Oriental Trading Company. At the time, you could get 500 bands for $50, which was a real bargain. They are even cheaper now. By going to their website, www.oriental trading.com, you could see their different choices on silly band types.

The silly bands were put into a large container in the library. Once the participants had read the book and completed the survey, they were allowed to pull seven bands out of the container; but they could keep only two of them. If they picked a number 7 band, then they got to keep all seven bands that they pulled out of the container, and they received another prize, which included a free paperback book, a free replacement student ID, or a free drink at one of our Read-A-Lattes. In retrospect, this could have been much easier if we had only purchased number bands. Even though it would have been more expensive, the students would not have been confused by the search idea. It seemed like a good idea to have them hunt for the 7, but the students did not really enjoy it as much as we thought they would.

DISTRIBUTE BOOKS

Having learned from the previous distribution from *Schooled* and *I,Q*, some of us changed our distribution method, while others decided to distribute in the same way. If you recall, *Schooled* was distributed through advisory classes and *I,Q* at a pep rally. Since the distribution of *Schooled* seemed more successful, I chose to go back to that method. The language arts teachers randomly chose a student in each of their classes and gave out the books on the launch date.

While this seemed like a good idea, some teachers did not remember until the next day. The video that I sent them to show did not work for some teachers, so this made it more difficult for the students to really get excited.

As before, some of the books were held back so they would be available at a later date. Then, as the semester progressed, books continued to be hidden in the hallway. Additionally, some were given to a teacher for her to read aloud with her students, hopefully to promote excitement among that entire group of students. If you do this, make sure that the teachers have read and *enjoyed* the book before reading it aloud to their students. Not everyone will like every book that you choose for the RIF program, and if you are encouraging a read aloud, you want to make sure that the reader enjoys the selection.

As with the other two titles, these books were signed in a similar fashion, but the message was pointed, "Will Jim find the 7th in time?" "When did you figure out what the 7th was? I figured it out on page __. No, I am not going to tell you because you will skip to that part. ;-)" "Enjoy the book!" The first message was better than the second, especially if you get writers' cramp. Of course, choosing an even shorter message also works. In the three years I have been running the RIF program, I have not noticed any difference between the students' responses for the books with a long note and the books with the short note. Since the shorter note was easier on me, that's the way I'll go in the future.

PROGRAMMING

Although the programming connections were not quite as obvious for this book as with the various themes in *Schooled*, we devised several different curricular events that engaged the students in the novel. Again, the geography program was fun to plan.

Since this book centered around a hunt, we planned a geocaching event. According to geocaching.com, "geocaching is a worldwide game of hiding and seeking treasure. A geocacher can place a geocache in the world, pinpoint its location using GPS technology and then share the geocache's existence and location online. Anyone with a GPS unit can then try to locate the geocache."

This may sound daunting, but it was a lot of fun. My original plan was to enlist teachers with iPhones to help, but any type of GPS device will work. This is a great time to ask in your school community if there are any experts who can help you with the event. More than likely, there is someone who has done it before and would be willing to help. We found we had a geocaching expert on campus, and this person set up all of the finds as well as the coordinates on the technology that our campus owns. Experience has shown me that one reason I get overwhelmed and stop offering programming is because I try to do everything myself. You never know when you might find a volunteer who has just been waiting for a prime opportunity to share expertise and experiences. As I tell the students, what is the worst thing that will happen? There will be no help; and I am no worse than when starting the planning phase.

To get started with designing your own geocaching event, join the geocaching community. It's free. Just go to geocaching.com and sign up. Then, you can see if there are caches in your area. If you have never done this before, use what is already available to you. We had caches in our area, and it was my plan to use them. It was fortunate to have someone in our school who was more than willing to set it up for the students. One valuable piece of advice that he gave to me was to check out the caches before going to them with students. Sometimes, caches can be old and not actually have any items inside the container. Since you want the students to have an interesting and fun experience, make sure that they are not disappointed the very first time they go on this type of adventure.

My own children were able to attend the event, and they loved it. They even worked on developing our family caching insignia. One thing you need to know is that when you take something from the cache, you should leave a marker of some kind. Interestingly, in the 2010–2011 Lone Star list, there was another book that had a geocaching component as well. This gave another a tie-in for another book and the list. The second novel is *North of Beautiful* by Justina Chen Headley. It is always helpful to tie two books together to show students real world connections, and when the students can do it for you, it is very satisfying.

For the math program, we tied math with reading by showing the students how to make a scytale such as was used in the book. A scytale is an encryption tool used to figure out a transpositional cipher. There are multiple ways to make scytales, and students may already know some of the methods; but two websites have good instructions. The first website comes from the PBS series, Zoom. Go to http://pbskids.org/zoom/activities/sci/scytalem essages.html and you'll find good instructions along with a materials list. You can also share this website with students who are not able to attend the event, but are very interested in the connections. Another website can be found at http://library.thinkquest .org/04oct/00451/scytale.htm. This website was designed by students and it is student-friendly. Offering two websites allows students to see two different viewpoints on the same topic.

Make sure that you try this out with various cylinders before working with students. It might be best to start with a message that was made using one of the cylinders. Then, encourage students to find the right cylinder to be able to read the message. This gives them a better view of what the protagonist of the book, Jim, went through when he was trying to decipher the message.

A movie program is always appealing to students because you can show it in the library and offer them popcorn. In a school setting, we do not always have the opportunity to show a film that directly relates to the book, so when I find a movie that ties in, I take advantage of the opportunity. When I read this book, I thought of the movie *The Sixth Sense*. However, it is rated PG-13 and we had students as young as 11, so I decided not to show it. I also saw some connections with the Scooby Doo movies, so I held a quick session with some of the students where we compared *The Hunt for the Seventh* with Scooby Doo. We had a great time with this goofy comparison.

Remember that if you show a movie with more than 25 students, you will need to get a license to show a movie for entertainment. As mentioned in Chapter 9, you can do this easily.

KEEPING TRACK

Again, a Google Doc was set up for students to complete once they finished the book. We designed a separate Google Doc that had a place for students to put who had the book and on what date. This allowed us to track the progress of the book, similarly to the

"Where is George?" campaign that tries to track the travels of a dollar bill. This was not successful because it was not fully publicized; so in the future, we may use a QR code and see if this can help track the books.

At this point, we've determined it's impossible to have 100 percent of the students complete an online form. However, since that is not the goal of the program, it is not where a great deal of effort should be spent. It's better to spend more time on making sure that everyone who wants to read the book gets the opportunity.

The students like to write their names in the front of the books. Many of the past books turn up with multiple signatures. A teacher found a book from our first year, and it had 34 signatures in it. Some of the students even wrote notes for the other readers. While you must be concerned with statistics to some extent, I'm sure the signatures in the book will be priceless to you as they were to me.

CULMINATING EVENT ACTIVITIES

Many of the programming ideas mentioned on the previous pages will also work as culminating event activities. If possible, conclude with an author visit so that the students have the chance to meet the person who wrote the book that has been the center of attention during the duration of the program. If that is not possible, as it wasn't for us this time, the alternative is to combine two of our favorite programs into the culminating event.

The activity "What's Cookin' @ Your Library" combines reading with two primal student interests—eating and competition. Students are shown connections to books through competitive cooking contests that highlight young adult fiction titles. After signing up for the event, they are assigned to teams, comprised of five people each, or you can also allow students to choose their groups. With the nature of the activity, the beginning organization is essential.

After students are broken into small groups, they are told to assign roles, or group tasks to each member. The roles are lead chef, ingredient person, spokesperson, plater, and judge. The lead chef listens to all suggestions, and is responsible for making the overall decisions. The ingredient person is the only person allowed to get ingredients at the central ingredient location. The plater is responsible for getting the plate(s) ready for the judges. The spokesperson is responsible for presenting the food along with the connection to the book to explain to the judges. The judge literally sits on the panel to rank the completed products. By having each group send a representative to judge, each group gets equal opportunity. The judges are given a simple rubric that is added together to decide the winner.

Once the group roles are determined, the groups are assigned a portion of a book or an entire book, depending on the overall topic and are given an instruction sheet. Then, students are given 20 minutes to prepare a dish based on the book parameters and the food parameters given to them. For instance, for *The Hunt for the Seventh*, the students were given the name of an object from the book, and they were told to create a dip with seven ingredients, no more, no less. After they created the dip and plated it for the judges, they wrote a 30–45 second explanation of the dip and how it related to the object given to them and the book as a whole. They are judged on the food as well as the connection to the book.

The object was to relate to the book. For example, for this book, the staircase was the object. So, a staircase was created from one block of cream cheese held together with toothpicks. Then, the (1) cream cheese was covered with (2) caramel sauce and (3) mini chocolate chips, served with (4) apple slices, (5) pretzels, (6) animal crackers, and (7) bananas. The significance of the staircase to the story was discussed, and participants were given instructions about how to write a 30-second connection to present to the judges.

Once the groups finish preparing their dishes, allow them to have five minutes to write about the connection to the book. This gives you time to get the judges in place, as well as getting the samples ready for the students. If possible, give each student a small taste of each of the dishes. Please check for food allergies before doing this. If you have enough adult help, students can taste at the same time as the judges. However, we have found it works best when they just receive a plate at the end with all of the samples on it. If all of the students are eating at the same time as the judges, they have a hard time keeping quiet. They want to give their two cents instead of letting the judges make their decisions.

Generally, we have 50–60 students participate in one session, so it is vital that they stay quiet for this portion. If you have a smaller number, you might able to have all of them complete rubrics, making sure that you have enough time to tally up the votes.

Here are two of the tools we used to publicize the event.

What's Cookin' @ Your Library?

Join us @ your library for an exciting event
combining reading and eating.

Upcoming Event:

- January 27, 2011: The Seventh Dimension

Space is limited.

Sign up early.

Check with Mrs. Kay if you have any questions concerning the event.

Figure 10.1   What's Cookin' @ Your Library Promotion #1

What's Cookin' @ Your Library?

The Seventh Dimension
Thursday, January 27th

3:30–5:00

**Work with a team to create a great dish
that combines cooking and reading.
No experience necessary.
To make this event meaningful,
space is limited.**

You must RSVP to attend this incredible event
by signing up @ Your Library today.

Figure 10.2   What's Cookin' @ Your Library Promotion #2

The following three pages are those that we gave to the students
when they walked into the event and got into their groups.

WHAT'S COOKIN' @ YOUR LIBRARY INSTRUCTIONS
THE SEVENTH DIMENSION

HERE IS YOUR MISSION:

You and your group will prepare a dip with seven ingredients (no more, no less) that connects to a certain portion of our feature book, *The Hunt for the Seventh*. You may make any type of dip that you want, but it can only have seven ingredients—including the dipping items. For example, if you make a dip that has five ingredients—then you need to have two items to serve with the dip.

PROCEDURES:

1. Get into your groups. Decide who will do the following jobs:
   > ingredient person
   > spokesperson
   > plate designer (who decides how to plate the food to give to the judges)
   > writer of the recipe
   > use special equipment if needed (i.e., if you need a microwave or some other special equipment, this person will use it.)

2. Look at your object choice connection to the book on the back of the recipe card at your table. You have three choices. Choose one and that will be your inspiration for your dip. (Example is the staircase.)

3. Talk among yourselves and decide what kind of dip you are going to make (sweet, hot, veggie, fruit, etc.).

4. Decide what ingredients you will need to make that dip. (You can ask the adult who is assigned to your group or Mrs. Kay for advice.) We have some limited appliances—ask the adult if you can do what you want with our limited resources before you start retrieving ingredients.

5. Once you have decided, send your ingredient person to the table to retrieve what you need (only the ingredient person is allowed at the ingredient table).

6. Begin making your dip.

7. Plate the dip for the judges. There will be 12 judges, and you will be given three plates to prepare for them. The rest will be given to our volunteers to prepare for the rest of the participants.

8. You will be given a note card with your connection to the book on it. On the other side, you will write down the ingredients that you used for your dip. Please don't forget to the put the name of your dip at the top.

9. While the volunteers are preparing the food for the participants, you will work on your 30–60 second explanation of how the dip fits with the piece of the book that you were given.

10. The entire group will prepare the explanation. This is a huge part of the judging—so be sure that your spokesperson explains well.

11. Everyone will be seated in front of the judges. The groups will present their dishes while everyone listens.

12. After the last group presents, every participant will receive samples from the different dips.

13. While the participants are sampling, the judges' votes will be tallied.

14. The winning groups will be awarded their prizes.

INGREDIENT CHOICES

cream cheese	cinnamon	ginger
sour cream	vanilla wafers	nutmeg
Eagle Brand milk	caramel sauce	seasoned salt
grated cheese	onion	cumin
chocolate chips	whipped cream	chickpeas
butterscotch chips	butterscotch sauce	sour cream
marshmallow creme	blackeyed peas	green onions
salt	apples	Velveeta
pepper	bananas	garlic powder
lemon	grapes	carrots
Splenda	cucumbers	yogurt
peppers	tomatoes	green onions
twisted pretzels	stick pretzels	crackers
Fritos	tortilla chips	
canned tomatoes	green chiles	

CONNECTION TO THE BOOK OBJECTS

garden (60)

bear (74)

blackboard (39)

ghost (44)

clock or clock tower

iron

statue (44)

stones (71)

Einstein (64)

School room (36)

secrets (79)

gravestones

forbidden chapel (63)

toy block (46)

weather vane (46)

accidents (67)

doll (78)

cat (79)

flashlight (79)

crown (79)

summer solstice (89)

sevenstone (69 and 94)

candles (37, 94, and 96)

willow basket (96)

numbers (23)

candlestick (43)

willow (95)

lantern (100)

chain

dumbwaiter

7

water (spring)

boat

lake

bells

hourglass

icehouse

Three of the objects above were put on the back of the recipe card. The students had the opportunity to choose which object they wanted from the three.

The students made excellent connections. Some of the dips were tastier than others, but all of them proved to be good. Here are the ingredients that the students used in their dips.

GROUP 1

(Object from book: lantern)

1 Tomatoes
2 Green pepper
3 Onion
4 Green chilies
5 Salt
6 Velveeta cheese
7 Tortilla chips

GROUP 2
BANANA BOATS

(Object from book: boat)

Ingredients:

1 Eagle Brand milk
2 Chocolate chips—melted
3 Marshmallow creme
4 Caramel sauce
5 Bananas
6 Vanilla wafers
7 Pretzel sticks

Combine the first four ingredients to make the dip. Serve by making boat from bananas, vanilla wafers, and pretzel sticks.

GROUP 3
SEVENSTONE FONDUE

(Object from book: sevenstone)

1 Cream cheese
2 Chocolate chips—melted
3 Marshmallow creme
4 Yogurt
5 Caramel sauce
6 Vanilla wafers
7 Pretzel sticks

Combine the first five ingredients. Put the dip in the middle with vanilla wafers surrounding as a sevenstone.

GROUP 4

(Object from book: ghost)

1 Tortilla chips
2 Tomatoes
3 Green bell peppers
4 Onion
5 Green chilies
6 Cream cheese
7 Fritos

Combine ingredients 2–5. On the dish, form the ghost from cream cheese. Surround the ghost with dip and chips.

GROUP 5
SECRET SURPRISE

(Object from book: secrets)

1 Cream cheese
2 Crushed vanilla wafers
3 Cinnamon
4 Whipped cream
5 Chocolate chips
6 Caramel sauce
7 Apples

Combine the first six ingredients to make the dip. Use apples to dip.

GROUP 6
BANANA CREAM BOX

(Object from book: toy block)

1 Cream cheese
2 Bananas
3 Cinnamon
4 Caramel sauce
5 Chocolate chips
6 Vanilla wafers
7 Stick pretzels

Combine the first five ingredients. Use wafers and pretzels to dip.

GROUP 7
AWESOMENESS GARDEN

(Object from book: garden)

1 Chocolate chips—melted
2 Marshmallow creme
3 butterscotch chips—melted
4 Whipped cream
5 butterscotch sauce
6 Pretzels
7 Vanilla wafers

Combine the first five ingredients. Use pretzels and vanilla wafers to dip. The judges could not get enough of this dip even after eating much of the other kinds. After discussing with the students about why this dip was so good, they exactly why it was the best tasting. They said that it must be the combination of those particular ingredients.

GROUP 8

(Object from book: 7)

1 Cream cheese
2 Chocolate chips—melted
3 Cinnamon
4 Caramel sauce
5 Whipped creme
6 Marshmallow creme
7 Apples

Combine the first six ingredients. Use apple to dip.

GROUP 9
CREAM CHEESE SURPRISE

(Object from book: numbers)

1 Apple
2 Lemon
3 Grapes
4 Cream cheese
5 Marshmallow creme
6 Ginger
7 Carrots

Combine cream cheese, marshmallow creme, lemon, and ginger. On three different plates, form cream cheese mixture into number shapes. Put apple, grapes, and carrots around the number-shaped dip.

GROUP 10
WINNING ENTRY
CHOCOLATE FONDUE

(Object from book: stones)

1 Melted chocolate chips
2 Whipped cream
3 Caramel
4 Cinnamon
5 Brown sugar
6 Pretzels
7 Vanilla wafers

Combine the first five ingredients. Use pretzels and vanilla wafers as dips. Place vanilla wafers around the dip to look like stones.

GROUP 11

(Object from book: lake)

1 Cream cheese
2 Marshmallow creme
3 Caramel
4 Cinnamon
5 Whipped creme
6 butterscotch sauce
7 Apples

Combine the first six ingredients. Use apples to dip.

If you do not feel up to the competitive food game, consider hosting a movie night with Scooby Doo or Casper or some other mystery, and serve some of these items as the refreshments. You could even play a game to see if students could guess the object based on the food; or you could choose one dip and make it with the group.

As with any other activity, you need to assess your strengths, your students' interests, and your volunteer capacity. Everyone can do something, just decide what you can do well and choose that.

One librarian, Lori Loranger, reported her comments from this year:

My school has participated in the Read It Forward program for the past three years. The first year was a great success! The students were excited when the program began and their excitement was reignited throughout the year with programs related to RIF. Being a new school, we did not have any money to get started at the beginning of the year so the kick-off was delayed until after our first Book Fair, so that we could fund the books and prizes. Our school could not afford the author visit, so instead we partnered with another school and transported students to the presentation by bus, which was much cheaper than having him come to our school. If I had the first year to do over, there is one thing I would do differently. Instead of keeping track of all of the students who had read the books, I had them sign a poster. This made it impossible to verify who had actually read the book when we had to draw names to determine who would go to the author visit. Plus, there were a few students who wrote inappropriate comments on the poster, which had to be removed.

It is obvious that each year, some ideas are more successful than others, but the concept of getting students to read remains a strong point for continuing for the fourth year. Every year brings with it challenges and insight to what works best with patrons. As we looked forward to our fourth year of RIF, we met together to discuss ways that we could expand the program by working with different groups of people.

Conclusion

When deciding on implementing a reading program for your patrons, you must consider what works well in your community. The best way to ensure that a program will work for you is to listen to your patrons informally through conversations, formally through surveys, and indirectly through circulation statistics. After speaking with my patrons, it became apparent that they enjoyed sharing with each other. As much as I like to affect as many people as possible, I know that collaborating with others will have a much greater impact.

Through this guide, you have the tools needed to implement a Read It Forward program by first choosing a great title. This point is very important for the success of the program. In this book, you have 25 examples that are wonderful books. If these titles are not what you do need, consider the authors and look at more titles written by them. Every author listed in this guide is successful and many of them have won multiple awards. By knowing your clientele and what would appeal most to them, you can pick a book that would suit everyone's needs.

Next, you must find the best way to obtain buy-in from your stakeholders. The beauty of this reading initiative is that you have multiple opportunities to involve others throughout the process—from the planning stages to the final events. When the stakeholders fully understand and support the program, you will have a much more successful time because you will reach more people. This type of reading initiative can be cost prohibitive if you do not plan well, so be sure that you spend time realizing your options for obtaining copies of the book. If your stakeholders are on board with the project, they may be able to help with the funding aspect as well.

Next, you want to promote excitement through various formats, and again, include as many people as possible. If you have a teacher or teachers with video producing skills, ask them to help you make an enticing video that will get the students excited about reading the book. You may have an art teacher who could help you design creative displays to promote the program. The title that you choose may bring new ideas for collaborative partners. Consider the plot of the book and seek those who have an interest in that area.

Keeping the students' interest in the program is vital to the success of the overall program. The different events that you offer in conjunction with the book will keep the students interested in reading the book or even wanting to read the book if they were not able to get a copy in the beginning. Let your programming events be plot-driven, but also listen to what your patrons want to drive the activities. You can develop the best connective activity to the book possible, but if your students or patrons are not interested in participating in the activity, you will not have the desired effect of reaching the most students. Additionally, keeping track of the students' progress is vital to knowing how many people have read the book and how many would like a copy of the book. Although it is not essential to have graphs and charts with the various people who have read the book, it does help in promoting the program in the future as well as promoting overall literacy. Remember that students do love to write cute notes, so allow them the opportunity to do this inside the cover of the book. This has proven to be the most successful way to get them to prove they had read the book.

Finally, the RIF program works best when you have a clear beginning and a clear end. If the author of the book is available for an author visit, that is a great culminating activity. However, this is not the only way to wrap up the program effectively. If a service project fits with the plot of the book, then that could be a very meaningful end to the program. Let the plot of the book as well as the climate of your library community drive this culminating event.

Although this book is about how to successfully implement a RIF program in your library, I want to stress how important it is to understand that the influence of this type of program cannot be measured in the length of one time. We are completing our fifth consecutive year of RIF, and I continue to have patrons ask for books from previous years. Patrons come back who have moved on and ask for a copy of the current RIF book. Additionally, many of the teachers who were here during the first and second years now read those books aloud to their students. Even though we are not highlighting those titles, the promotion continues.

In my library, the RIF program has developed a climate of sharing literature with each other. Even when I am busy with one student to find the right book, the other students will come in and recommend titles to each other. Honestly, that is what we want to see happen in our libraries and in our communities. To affect change in our world, we need to read more, and one great way to do that is to provide our patrons with the tools to share literature with each other. Choose a great book, share it with others, and show others how to do that as well.

Appendix: Annotated List

The next pages provide more titles that would be excellent choices for a RIF program. Some brainstorming ideas for programming and curricular connections help you initiate the planning stages for a RIF initiative with these books. In no way is this list exhaustive, but it is intended to provide starting ideas that will launch a RIF program.

TITLE:

Deuker, Carl. *Gym Candy*. Boston: Houghton Mifflin, 2007.

RECOMMENDED AGE FOR THIS RIF PLACEMENT:

High School or Upper Middle School grades

SUMMARY OF BOOK:

Gym Candy is an excellent sports book about Mick Johnson, a freshman wanting to play on the varsity football team. At first, he works very hard in the gym and refuses the trainer's advice to take steroids; however, after a time, Mick gives in to the pressure to become bigger, stronger, and faster through taking the drugs. This novel does an excellent job of showing how a seemingly good kid with his priorities right can still make a bad decision. Deuker does a great job of showing how one bad decision can lead to many more, and he does not hold back on the explanation of the side effects.

On first glance, it would appear that this book is just about steroids, but there is more to this story. Mick feels the pressure to be the best from his father, who won many sports awards during his football career. The sports story, along with the cautionary tale about steroids, would make this a good choice just on that merit, but the father–son story makes this an excellent choice.

Programming Possibilities:

1. Bringing in a speaker who will discuss the dangers of steroid use.
2. Sponsoring a powder puff football game.
3. Sponsoring a video/book trailer contest.
4. Team up with Special Olympics to aid them in getting volunteers for one of their meets.
5. Have a paper football contest. Yes, high school boys would love doing that.
6. During Red Ribbon Week, you could team up with that committee to promote the book along with the other programs they offer.
7. Sponsor a health fair where experts are brought in to talk about healthy choices through eating and exercise.

Curricular Connections:

Health: drugs and side effects of steroids

Science: biology, how drugs like steroids can affect the body

Athletics: During football season, you have an automatic tie-in from the library to the football field. Make special spirit signs for the football team about working hard and staying true to themselves.

Math: measuring muscle mass, weight, and so on

Prolific Author:

Deuker has written several young adult novels with a sports background. According to his website, he is available for author visits both in person and virtually through Skype.

TITLE:

Cooney, Caroline B. *Code Orange*. New York: Delacorte, 2005.

RECOMMENDED AGE FOR THIS RIF PLACEMENT:

Middle School

SUMMARY OF BOOK:

Code Orange is a great mystery novel about a sophomore, Mitty Blake, who has decided that everything he needs can be found on the internet. He is a carefree guy who does not want to work too hard for anything. However, he is interested in something or at least someone—his girlfriend, Olivia. Olivia is in Advanced Biology, so Mitty signed up for the class as well. The teacher assigns each student a disease to study, but they cannot do their beginning research online. Mitty finds an old medical book that has an envelope inside containing two scabs. Mitty touches them, of course; then he begins to wonder if has caught the disease, which just happens to be smallpox. Mitty then has decisions to make, such as who he can trust and what he needs to do if he does indeed have the disease. This is a page-turner worthy of your time.

Programming Possibilities:

1. Invite a doctor to speak to students about infectious diseases.
2. Have a "What's Cookin' @ Your Library" (See chapter 10 for details) event with orange being the secret ingredient.
3. Host a Pandemic game. The board game allows players to try to find the cure for four different diseases before the world's population is wiped out. The online game allows players to use the diseases as weapons of mass destruction.

Curricular Connections:

Science: infectious diseases

Language Arts: research project—specifically source verification

Social Studies: pandemics in the news

Math: probability of how the world's population would be affected in a pandemic

Prolific Author:

Caroline Cooney has written more than 90 novels. She no longer visits schools, but is a great example of a prolific author.

TITLE:

Mikaelsen, Ben. *Touching Spirit Bear.* New York: HarperCollins, 2001.

RECOMMENDED AGE FOR THIS RIF PLACEMENT:

Middle School

SUMMARY OF BOOK:

Cole Matthews is an angry teen who loses control and attacks another boy. Garvey, a Tlingit parole officer, offers Cole an alternative called Circle Justice, which is a system where the offender, the victim, and the community come together to find a solution for the offender. Through this, Cole is sentenced to one year on an island where he gets more than he bargained for as he is left to survive on his own. This story is a great one that provides the reader with a wonderful journey of self-discovery and forgiveness that is wrought with truth.

Programming Possibilities:

1. Invite a Native American speaker to explain how Circle Justice can work.
2. Create totem poles.
3. Invite a speaker from the Anti-Defamation League's No Place for Hate to discuss tolerance with students.
4. Create a peace garden that includes peaceful messages about the patrons' life circles.
5. Host a friendship bracelet workshop, inviting students to work with students they do not know.

Curricular Connections:

Social Studies: Students can have a trial where they decide Cole's fate.

Language Arts: Create a Google lit trip to map Cole's journey from Minnesota to Alaska.

Science: Study about the habitat on the island.

Prolific Author:

Ben Mikaelsen has written nine young adult novels. Mikaelsen is available for author visits, either in person or through teleconferencing.

TITLE:

Palacio, R. J. *Wonder*. New York: Alfred A. Knopf, 2012.

RECOMMENDED AGE FOR THIS RIF PLACEMENT:

Elementary, Middle School, High School

SUMMARY OF BOOK:

August Pullman, or Auggie, was born with a facial deformity. His mom has homeschooled him, but she has decided that he needs to attend school with other children. Auggie must now face the challenge of going to school with students who may not be able to get past his appearance. This novel is told in multiple voices, so the reader gets a real sense of everyone's feelings throughout the story.

Programming Possibilities:

1. Star Wars Themed Party—have everyone come as their favorite character.
2. Encourage everyone to pledge to choose kind by going to choosekind. tumblr.com.
3. Family movie night to celebrate familial relationships. For middle school, *Simon Birch* or *The Ant Bully* would be good connective movies.

Curricular Connections:

Science: Explore genetics, specifically Treacher-Collins Syndrome.

Social Studies: Develop monthly precepts for the whole school.

Language Arts: Points of view

Prolific Author:

This is R. J. Palacio's debut novel. Even though it is her first, it is fantastic and would make a great book for an RIF program.

TITLE:

Meyer, Marissa. *Cinder*. New York: Feiwel and Friends, 2012.

RECOMMENDED AGE FOR THIS RIF PLACEMENT:

Middle School, High School

SUMMARY OF BOOK:

Cinder is a new kind of Cinderella story. This story takes place in a post–World War IV place called New Beijing, where Cinder is a cyborg teen mechanic. One day, Cinder is in her shop admiring her new foot that she just purchased when in walks Prince Kai. He has a robot that he wants her to fix for him. Since he has his own mechanics at the castle, she questions his motives. He assures her that they are busy, and he needs the robot for sentimental reasons. Cinder takes the job and soon finds that there is more than meets the eye for the prince and for her.

Programming Possibilities:

1. Fairy tale party: Everyone comes as their favorite fairy tale character.
2. Movie night: Watch a version of *Cinderella* and compare/contrast this story.
3. Cyborg blaster game

Curricular Connections:

Social studies: Government of the society, monarchy, and so on

Science: genetics, cybernetics

Language Arts: fairy tales/point of view

Prolific Author:

Cinder is Marissa Meyer's debut novel; however, *Cinder* is the first installment in a four-part series.

TITLE:

Lane, Andrew. *Death Cloud*. New York: Farrar Straus Giroux, 2011.

RECOMMENDED AGE FOR THIS RIF PLACEMENT:

Upper Elementary, Middle School

SUMMARY OF BOOK:

Death Cloud is about Sherlock Holmes's first case when he was 14 years old, at least as Andrew Lane has imagined it. Sherlock is sent to stay with relatives over the summer holiday, and he notices that there are two mysterious deaths that have a common cloud around them. Sherlock must figure out what is going on before anyone else dies. This book offers a fun view of what Sherlock might have been as a teen.

Programming Possibilities:

1. Mystery in the library
2. Sherlock Holmes party
3. Mystery book activity
4. Movie Night: Possibly show old black and white movies of Sherlock Holmes.
5. What's Cookin' @ Your Library Event, with honey or food beginning with the letter B as your secret ingredient

Curricular Connections:

Science: killer bees

Language Arts: Analyze the different archetypes in the book; compare/contrast with original Arthur Conan Doyle books.

Math: Logic problems

Prolific Author:

Lane has written 20 books. *Death Cloud* is the first book in the *Young Sherlock Holmes* series.

TITLE:

Cody, Matthew. *Powerless*. New York: Alfred A. Knopf, 2009.

RECOMMENDED AGE FOR THIS RIF PLACEMENT:

Upper Elementary, Middle School

SUMMARY OF BOOK:

Daniel's family moves to Nobles Green, where he meets some kids with superpowers. In fact, all of these kids have superpowers, but he finds that they are in danger of losing these powers when they turn 13. Even though Daniel does not possess any superpowers, he brings a clever wit to the table to help them learn why they lose their powers at the age of 13.

Programming Possibilities:

1. Design your own superhero contest.
2. Movie night: Watch *Sky High*
3. Video contest of what the best superpower would be and how they would use it—for good or for evil
4. What's Cookin @ Your Library event: foods must have 13 components

Curricular Connections:

Science: genetics/superpowers

Language Arts: Write position paper on why the age 13 was such a pivotal piece in the book.

Prolific Author:

Matthew Cody has written three young adult novels. He is available for school visits.

TITLE:

Sonnenblick, Jordan. *Drums, Girls, & Dangerous Pie*. New York: Scholastic, 2005.
AND
Sonnenblick, Jordan, and Marijka Kostiw. *After Ever After*. New York: Scholastic, 2010.

RECOMMENDED AGE FOR THIS RIF PLACEMENT:

Middle School

SUMMARY OF BOOK:

These two titles are companion books. In the first title, *Drums, Girls, & Dangerous Pie*, Steven is a 13-year-old boy whose four-year-old brother, Jeffrey, is diagnosed with leukemia. Told from Steven's perspective, readers see a firsthand glimpse of what it is like for a close family member to be diagnosed with a life-threatening disease. In *After Ever After*, readers get to hear Jeffrey's perspective as the 13-year-old cancer survivor. Steven is not around in this volume since he has gone to Africa to find himself. These titles work well when partnered for RIF since they show two different perspectives nine years apart. The characters are genuine and caring.

Programming Possibilities:

1. Host a family event where you raise money for a nonprofit organization that benefits cancer victims/survivors.

   The first book has a benefit concert, and the second book has a bike race.
2. Ask cancer survivors to talk to students about their experiences.
3. Make pillows for cancer patients.
4. What's Cookin' @ Your Library Event—must include at least one of the ingredients for dangerous pie.

Curricular Connections:

Science: diseases

Math: Create a budget for a benefit concert; find out the costs for a critically ill patient.

Band/Orchestra: concerts

Prolific Author:

Jordan Sonnenblick has written several young adult novels. He is available for author visits.

TITLE:

Hobbs, Will. *Take Me to the River*. New York: Harper, 2011.

RECOMMENDED AGE FOR THIS RIF PLACEMENT:

Middle School

SUMMARY OF BOOK:

Dylan Sands is going to paddle down the Rio Grande for the first time with his cousin, Rio, and his uncle. However, Dylan's uncle went to Alaska for work, so it appears that the trip is off. Rio and Dylan decide to venture out on their own, only to be caught out in Hurricane Dolly. In this high-paced adventure, Dolly is not the only storm these two will face. They also meet a man named Carlos who is camping with a seven-year-old boy, but this boy looks very scared. Dylan and Rio have to figure out how to navigate around all of the trials they face as they go down the river.

Programming Possibilities:

1. Host an outdoor survival specialist.
2. Organize a food/clothing drive.
3. Organize a clean-up effort at nearby creeks/lakes, if applicable.
4. Make survival bracelets.
5. Host a survival event where each group gets a small amount of money to buy food in a convenience store to last a week.

Curricular Connections:

Science: weather

Social Studies: geography

Prolific Author:

Will Hobbs has written more than 20 young adult adventure books. He is available for author visits.

TITLE:

Flinn, Alex. *Beastly*. New York: HarperTeen, 2007.

RECOMMENDED AGE FOR THIS RIF PLACEMENT:

Upper Middle School, High School

SUMMARY OF BOOK:

Kyle Kingsbury had it all—looks, money, attitude until he made the wrong girl angry. After he humiliates her, she casts a spell on him that turns him into a creature who is just as ugly on the outside as his personality is on the inside. Kyle has two years to break the curse by finding someone who will love him despite his appearance. In walks Lindy, a beautiful girl, who can save him from this life-altering fate. In this re-telling of *Beauty and the Beast*, Flinn brings in modern touches that add to the story. For instance, Kyle joins an online chat group with other people dealing with similar issues such as *The Little Mermaid* and *The Frog Prince*.

Programming Possibilities:

1. Host a fractured fairytale reading party.
2. Host a movie night for a different version of *Beauty and the Beast*.
3. Host a movie night for the film *Beastly*.
4. Read another retelling of *Beauty and the Beast*.

Curricular Connections:

Language Arts: fairytales
Science: roses

Prolific author:

Flinn has written several young adult novels. Many of them are fairytale retellings.

TITLE:

Lupica, Mike. *Heat*. New York: Philomel, 2006.

RECOMMENDED AGE FOR THIS RIF PLACEMENT:

Upper Elementary, Middle School

SUMMARY OF BOOK:

Michael Arroyo is a 13-year-old Cuban boy who dreams of playing baseball in the Major Leagues. Different from other 13-year-olds, Michael actually has a shot at it. He is really talented, but he has a serious problem. His father has died, and he and his brother are living on their own. They do not want to be separated, so they are keeping their father's death a secret. Michael and his brother, Carlos, must figure out how they will get his birth certificate from Cuba without letting their secret out for the world to know.

Programming Possibilities:

1. Movie night with *The Perfect Game* or *Mickey*.
2. Host a faculty/student donkey baseball tournament.
3. Host college, minor, or major league athletes to talk about sportsmanship, teamwork, and so on.

Curricular Connections:

Physical Education: baseball

Social Studies: history of baseball, geography

Math: Develop problems about how much it costs to go to a Yankees game with refreshment, souvenirs.

Prolific Author:

Mike Lupica is a great sports writer who made his way into the young adult field with Travel Team. Now, he has written several young adult sports novels.

TITLE:

Flanagan, John. *The Ruins of Gorlan*. New York: Philomel, 2005.

RECOMMENDED AGE FOR THIS RIF PLACEMENT:

Upper Elementary, Middle School

SUMMARY OF BOOK:

Will is a precocious 15-year-old who is anxiously awaiting Choosing Day, where he will be assigned to a master for his training. Will wants to be a knight, but he is apprenticed to a mysterious Ranger named Halt. Will soon finds out that the Rangers have been protecting the kingdom through secretive operations for years. Will must protect the kingdom from the evil magic that threatens the livelihood of his people.

Programming Possibilities:

1. Host a bow and arrow competition.
2. Host a speaker that works for the CIA.
3. Host a game day that includes alternate realities.

4. Host a scavenger hunt.

5. Host a gaming activity where patrons can play games on the series website: www.rangersapprentice.com.

Prolific Author:

John Flanagan has written 10 books in this series, and he is now writing a new series entitled *The Brotherband Chronicles*.

TITLE:

Shulman, Mark. *Scrawl: A Novel*. New York: Roaring Brook, 2010.

RECOMMENDED AGE FOR THIS RIF PLACEMENT:

Middle School, High School

SUMMARY OF BOOK:

Tod Munn is the stereotypical school bully. He has gotten in trouble for vandalizing at his school, but while his buddies must endure hours of outside cleanup duty, Tod has been sentenced to detention with the school guidance counselor. In this detention, he must write in a journal. In fact, the entire book is told through Tod's journal. In this journal, we find out what really happened in the vandalizing episode as well as how Tod came to be known as a school bully instead of the bright student he seemingly is, given his journal entries.

Programming Possibilities:

1. Host a dressed-up journal event where students upcycle journals.

2. Host a clean-up day where participants choose an area where they clean up outside.

3. If timing works out, host an activity in conjunction with National Bullying Prevention Month—October.

4. Host a cyberbullying prevention workshop.

Curricular Connections:

Social Studies: conflict resolution between countries

Language Arts: journal entries

Prolific Author:

Mark Shulman has written several books, including picture books and younger chapter books.

TITLE:

Draper, Sharon M. *Out of My Mind*. New York: Atheneum for Young Readers, 2010.

RECOMMENDED AGE FOR THIS RIF PLACEMENT:

Middle School, High School

SUMMARY OF BOOK:

Melody is not your average fifth grader. She has cerebral palsy, which affects her body; therefore, she cannot walk, talk, or feed herself. She is a brilliant person, but the people in her school do not realize it until she gets Elvira, her Medi-Talker computer. Then, she is able to let people know what has been going on in her world. This novel gives readers the opportunity to understand what a person with physical difficulties feels and thinks.

Programming Possibilities:

1. Host an event where participants must take on a physical disability, such as being in a wheelchair, being blind, and so on.
2. Host a party for students with physical disabilities along with students that do not have physical disabilities.
3. Host a Wii or Xbox Kinect game time and talk about how it would be different if we could not control our actions.

Curricular Connections:

Science: cerebral palsy and other genetic disorders

Math: statistics for how many children are born with cerebral palsy or other genetic disorders

Prolific Author:

Sharon Draper has written multiple award-winning novels that reach the hearts of readers. Draper is available for school visits, but you must book her well in advance.

TITLE:

Riordan, Rick. *The Maze of Bones. 39 Clues.* New York: Scholastic, 2008.

RECOMMENDED AGE FOR THIS RIF PLACEMENT:

Elementary

SUMMARY OF BOOK:

Grace Cahill leaves behind a challenge for her family. Each member of her family who is named in the will may inherit $1 million immediately, or he or she may receive the first of 39 clues to lead them to a treasure beyond measure. Some of the older members of the family take the money and leave, but other members decide to take the challenge. There are five sects of the family, and each of the sects represents a different type of personality. Some of the family are much more loving than others, but all of them are in a race to see who will be able to figure out the 39 clues to get to the secret family stash.

Programming Possibilities:

1. Reveal book with students in an assembly and have envelopes under some of the chairs. The students who have an envelope will be the ones who receive the book.
2. Treasure hunt
3. Grandparents' Day event, where grandparents narrate stories of their school days.

Curricular Connections:

Social Studies: family tree; geography around the world

Math: problems about how much money there would be in the family fortune if everyone had taken $1 million

Language Arts: Google lit trip

Prolific Author:

Rick Riordan is the author of this volume in the *39 Clues* series of books. He also designed the plan for the rest of the series even though they were written by other people. Additionally, he wrote the wildly popular *Percy Jackson* series. Riordan is available for author visits.

TITLE:

Carter, Ally. *Heist Society*. New York: Disney/Hyperion, 2010.

RECOMMENDED AGE FOR THIS RIF PLACEMENT:

Middle School

SUMMARY OF BOOK:

Katarina Bishop wants to leave the family business behind, but this decision is not hers alone. Kat's family business is thievery, specifically priceless art, and there are people who value her talent. Her father is accused of stealing a famous criminal's paintings, and his life is in danger. Kat is convinced that her father is innocent of this crime, so she puts together a team to find the paintings and return them to their owner in a two-week time period.

Programming Possibilities:

1. Mystery in the library
2. Host an artist to talk to the students about the fine points of painting.
3. Host an art event where students get to design a painting themselves.
4. Design a mural for your library that you can work on together.
5. Host a heist Sudoku party—available online at author's website.

Curricular Connections:

Math: economics
Art: history
Social Studies: art history, geography

Prolific Author:

Ally Carter is the author of the *Gallagher Girls* series, and Heist Society is the first book in the *Heist Society* novels.

TITLE:

Van Draanen, Wendelin. *The Running Dream*. New York: Alfred A. Knopf, 2011.

RECOMMENDED AGE FOR THIS RIF PLACEMENT:

Middle School, High School

SUMMARY OF BOOK:

Jessica is a runner. She loves everything about running, and she is thrilled to be a part of the school's track team. However, the track team is in a terrible auto accident, and Jessica loses her leg. She receives a prosthetic leg, but it is not quite the same. She tries to run with it, but it is painful. Now, Jessica must figure out what is really important to her as she befriends a girl with cerebral palsy, Rosa, who has never walked.

Programming Possibilities:

1. Host a speaker with prosthetics.
2. Host a game where each player must be without a limb.
3. Host a running event to raise money for a good cause for your school/community.

Curricular Connections:

Physical education: running
Science: prosthetics

Prolific Author:

Wendelin Van Draanen has written many wonderful novels, including the *Sammy Keyes* series as well as *Flipped*, which has recently been adapted to film.

TITLE:

Shusterman, Neal. *The Schwa Was Here*. New York: Dutton Children's, 2004.

RECOMMENDED AGE FOR THIS RIF PLACEMENT:

Upper Elementary, Middle School

SUMMARY OF BOOK:

Anthony Bonano, Antsy, is fascinated by a kid at school named Calvin Schwa. Calvin is a boy that no one ever notices. No matter what he does, people do not seem to see him. Antsy decides this is a perfect way to make some money, so he teams up with Calvin and begins taking bets about what Calvin can get away with. This works pretty well until old man Crawley catches them trying to steal a dog bowl. Crawley requires them to do some community service to make up for their misdeeds, and that is when these two team up with Lexie, Crawley's blind granddaughter, who sees Calvin for the great kid that he is.

Programming Possibilities:

1. Invisible ink workshop
2. Camouflage Day
3. Schwa Effect Workshop: see how many ideas people can come up to see if the schwa could be seen.
4. Schwa Story Swapping: begin with Shusterman's personal story as told in Award acceptance speech—then everyone share theirs to see who has the best one.

Curricular Connections:

Science: animals hiding in nature; scientific method

Social Studies: discuss times when you want to be invisible

Prolific Author:

Neal Shusterman has written more than 20 young adult novels ranging in genre from suspense to realistic fiction. He is available for school visits.

TITLE:

Shusterman, Neal. *Full Tilt: A Novel*. New York: Simon & Schuster for Young Readers, 2003.

RECOMMENDED AGE FOR THIS RIF PLACEMENT:

Middle School

SUMMARY OF BOOK:

Blake is a 16-year-old boy who has always followed the rules, which is very different from his younger brother, Quinn. Blake and Quinn attend a carnival where they meet Cassandra, who invites them to a very different kind of carnival. Blake has no intention of going to that carnival that does not open until midnight, but Quinn takes his ticket. When Quinn is found in a comatose state later that night, Blake knows immediately what he has done. Now, it is up to Blake and his two friends to go to the carnival to save Quinn from himself. However, they must ride a certain number of rides to make it out, or they will be stuck there. As if that is not enough to make you want to read this page-turner, the rides represent one's worst nightmares.

Programming Possibilities:

1. Go to an amusement park.
2. Host an amusement park-themed party.
3. Movie night: watch a suspense movie.

Curricular Connections:

Science: Design roller coasters.

Math: Create infographic with stats about amusement park attendance or favorite park rides.

Prolific Author:

Neal Shusterman has written more than 20 young adult novels, ranging in genre from suspense to realistic fiction. He is available for school visits.

TITLE:

Colfer, Eoin. *The Wish List*. New York: Miramax/Hyperion for Children, 2003.

RECOMMENDED AGE FOR THIS RIF PLACEMENT:

Middle School

SUMMARY OF BOOK:

Meg Finn is a 14-year-old troubled teen who is thrown out of her house by her stepfather after her mother died. She partners with Belch, a real troublemaker, who convinces her that they need to rob an elderly man, Lowrie McCall. McCall pulls out a shotgun; Belch sicks his pitbull on McCall; Meg runs away; Belch runs after her with the shotgun. Then, things get really bad. Belch shoots in the air, and they happen to be under a gas tank. They are killed immediately, and Belch is on his way to hell. Meg, however, is in a different state. She cannot go to hell or heaven; she is truly in limbo. Now, she is given the wonderful opportunity to go back to earth to do enough good deeds to get to heaven. Beelzebub has other ideas because he wants her in hell, so he sends Belch and the dog back to earth to foil her plans.

Programming Possibilities:

1. Play choices game, where participants must pick one side or the other about a controversial subject.
2. Host a "Would you rather" event.
3. Wish List writing event: keep them and send to students at a later date in the future.

Curricular Connections:

Social Studies: religions

Science: experiments where one ingredient makes the difference for the compound

Prolific Author:

Eoin Colfer is the author of several series, including *The Artemis Fowl* series.

TITLE:

Van Draanen, Wendelin. *Runaway*. New York: Alfred A. Knopf, 2006.

RECOMMENDED AGE FOR THIS RIF PLACEMENT:

Middle School, High School

SUMMARY OF BOOK:

Holly is a 12-year-old who has seen much heartache in her life. She is in her fifth foster home, and she has not been treated well in any of them. She feels like her only option is to run away. Holly decides that to truly be rid of the problems, she needs to go across the country. She gets on a bus and goes to a completely different place. Holly starts over, but she writes to her English teacher through poetry in her journal. In *Runaway*, readers get to experience what it feels like to be homeless and, quite frankly, hopeless until Holly meets kind people who show her how life can be when you find people you can trust.

Programming Possibilities:

1. Service project for homeless shelter
2. Supply drive for animal shelter
3. Coat drive for local serving centers

Curricular Connections:

Math: Graph how many runaways are in the United States.

Science: climate and what would be needed for survival without shelter

Prolific Author:

Wendelin Van Draanen has written many wonderful novels, including the *Sammy Keyes* series as well as *Flipped*, which has recently been adapted to film.

TITLE:

Mulligan, Andy. *Trash*. Oxford: David Fickling, 2010.

RECOMMENDED AGE FOR THIS RIF PLACEMENT:

Middle School, High School

SUMMARY OF BOOK:

In an unnamed Third World country, Raphael, Gardo, and Rat are dumpsite boys. They literally survive by what they can salvage in the trash they find in their dumpsite. One day, Raphael discovers a small leather bag, and he realizes that it is worth far more than the money inside it. All three boys decide not to tell the authorities because they are not sure who they can trust. As the story unfolds, the boys find out quickly that this is no ordinary wallet, and they must decide whether revealing the truth is worth the consequences.

Programming Possibilities:

1. Host an upcycle trash craft event.
2. Composting activity
3. Begin recycling of wrappers and other materials in the community.
4. T-shirt bag activity

Curricular Connections:

Social Studies: Third World country study

Math: economics

Science: study students' trash contents

Prolific Author:

Mulligan has written the *Ribblestrop* series in addition to *Trash*.

TITLE:

Johnson, Angela. *The First Part Last*. New York: Simon & Schuster for Young Readers, 2003.

RECOMMENDED AGE FOR THIS RIF PLACEMENT:

High School

SUMMARY OF BOOK:

Bobby and Nia are happy high school students until Nia reveals something to Bobby on his 16th birthday that changes their lives forever. Nia is pregnant, and they have to figure out what they are going to do. People are telling them to put the baby up for adoption, but Bobby cannot bear the thought of that once the baby, Feather, is born. So, Bobby takes Feather home and figures out quickly how hard parenthood is for a new parent.

Curricular Connections:

Science/Health: study of eclampsia
Math: statistics about teen pregnancy

Prolific Author:

Angela Johnson has written several award-winning books.

Index

About the Author

LINDA KAY is a middle school librarian at Ridgeview Middle School, Round Rock, Texas. A 20-year veteran educator, Kay received a bachelor's degree from Abilene Christian University and a master's degree from Texas Tech University, both in communication studies. She also earned a master's degree in library science from the University of North Texas.

One of her joys in life is finding the right title for each individual that walks into the library. Her belief is that everyone is a reader at heart—he or she just needs to find the right book to ignite that love of reading.